PATHS OF A PRODIGAL

"**Paths of a Prodigal** *is a wise and wonderful book!"*

KEN WILBER, author of
Sex, Ecology, Spirituality and
A Brief History of Everything

"*Where was this book when I needed it years ago?* **Paths of a
Prodigal** *is one of the wisest descriptions of the spiritual journey
written in recent years. For anyone interested in exploring the mystical aspects of Christianity, this book will be exceedingly helpful."*

LARRY DOSSEY, M.D., author of
Prayer Is Good Medicine and
Healing Words

"*This is a book full of insights, all of which speak to us directly.
Humor and essential goodness, which are often harder to maintain than flashes of enlightenment, highlight the author's family
life and his life in the world. This is a thoughtful and deeply
spiritual book."*

ANNE BANCROFT, author of
The Spiritual Journey and
The Luminous Vision

PATHS OF A PRODIGAL

Exploring the Deeper Reaches
of Spiritual Living

Richard G. Young, Ph.D.

Foreword by

Larry Dossey, M.D.

PUBLISHED FOR THE PAUL BRUNTON
PHILOSOPHIC FOUNDATION BY

LARSON PUBLICATIONS

International Standard Book Number: 0-943914-81-7
Library of Congress Catalog Card Number: 97-70330

Published for the Paul Brunton Philosophic Foundation by
Larson Publications
4936 NYS Route 414
Burdett, NY 14818 USA

04 03 02 01 00 99 98 97

10 9 8 7 6 5 4 3 2 1

Permission applications are in progress as required
for reprinting of material under copyright.

For Nancy, Chad, and Adam
Without whose loving attentions
this book would have been written
in about half the time

For Gary G. Collins, Ph.D.
Teacher, mentor, and friend:
"I shall never get over Thee"

And for Thomas Merton
Who turned me around and said,
"Go home!"

ACKNOWLEDGMENTS

SOMEONE said that writing a book is easy. All you have to do is sit down at your desk, take out a pen, and open a vein. Listed below are a few of the people who willingly bled with me. I did it because I had to. They did it because they cared.

My deepest debt of love and gratitude is to Nancy, my wife of twenty-five years. Not only did she live through this entire process with a distracted and often moody husband, but she read every word of every draft and graciously offered many helpful suggestions (none of which I received very graciously).

Bruce Langford is my partner and friend, and a gifted writer in his own right. He took what I believed was the final draft of *Paths of a Prodigal* and slashed and burned it (okay, so I'm a little verbose). Don't get me wrong, he was always kind and loving about it. But each new editorial conference would bring tears to my eyes. He was able to take a loose collection of rambling stories and reflections and craft them into an articulate whole—and I love him for it.

My publisher, Paul Cash, edited the final version of this book with such care and precision that I am in complete awe of his editorial talent. He literally "made the rough places smooth." His wife, Amy, continues to do a marvelous job of bringing attention to my work. Her suggestions and support early in this project were invaluable.

I also wish to thank Ken Wilber, Anne Bancroft, Alan Cohen, and Sheldon Kramer for reading the manuscript and offering support in a variety of ways.

Finally, I need to express my most heartfelt thanks to Larry Dossey, M.D. He offered a young writer something far more valuable than just his support and encouragement—he offered his friendship.

CONTENTS

These are the thoughts of all men in all ages and lands,
    they are not original with me,
If they are not yours as much as mine they are nothing
    or next to nothing,
If they do not enclose everything they are next to
    nothing,
If they are not the riddle and the untying of the riddle
    they are nothing,
If they are not just as close as they are different
    they are nothing.

WALT WHITMAN

FOREWORD

by Larry Dossey, M.D.

HUMANKIND is literally sitting on the edge of tomorrow. In a few short years, we will journey together into a new century and a new millennium. What will life be like on the other side of the year 2000? Will we usher in an epoch of spiritual awakening and healing, as so many have hoped, or will we continue the materialism and spiritual cynicism of our time? Will we learn to live in harmony with nature and in unity with one another, or will we find more efficient ways to ravage Gaia and exploit our neighbor?

As we wait quietly and expectantly in the pre-dawn stillness of the coming age, we can begin to perceive the subtle currents of change in the early morning mist. For example, intercessory prayer, once considered primitive and superstitious by most scientists, is receiving considerable scientific attention and validation. Many enlightened physicians, psychologists, and other health care professionals now routinely pray for their patients and clients. This is because they have been impressed by the growing number of empirical studies affirming a positive effect of intercessory prayer and have proven the efficacy of prayer repeatedly in their own clinical practice. Indeed, the day may come when it is considered medical malpractice for physicians to withhold prayer from their patients.

There are other signs of change as well. Consider the fact that more and more people in the West are looking beyond the sectarian concerns and moralistic doctrines of their particular religious traditions in an attempt to rediscover the essential *experience* of spiritual truth that is common to all faiths. It is no longer enough for them to *believe* in God, especially a god who has been described only in terms of theological concepts and anthropomorphic images. Like Moses on the mountain, they want to *know* the Absolute Reality directly for themselves, without conceptual mediation or verbal explanation. As a result of this intense desire for a personal and transformative experience of the Divine, many people find themselves consulting the perennial wisdom of Eastern religious traditions to guide and inspire their Christian spiritual practice. This growing interest in Eastern mysticism and transpersonal development serves as both a challenge to traditional Christianity and the very hope for its renewed relevance and vitality.

To meet this challenge in the years ahead, Western Christianity must return to the experiential knowledge of union with the Absolute, a knowledge spoken of so eloquently by the Apostle Paul and the author of the Gospel of John. Individual Christians will need to explore their own rich tradition of mystical and contemplative spirituality and then integrate the universal, esoteric truth they discover with the revealed truth of other religions. Only then can they return to the living Source of Christ's teachings on spiritual transformation and universal brotherhood and renew their message of hope and reconciliation to the world.

Paths of a Prodigal is a gentle and moving account of one man's attempt to do that in his own experience. Richard Young has written a book of remarkable clarity, honesty, and good humor. It is one of the wisest descriptions of the spiritual journey written in recent years. His heart-felt stories of faith and light reveal his deep desire to know God "face-to-face," and to rediscover the contemplative core of his own spiritual tradition. For anyone interested in exploring the experiential and mystical aspects of Christianity in preparation for the new millennium, Richard's book will be exceedingly helpful.

LARRY DOSSEY, M.D., author of
Prayer is Good Medicine, Healing Words,
and *Recovering the Soul*

FOREWORD

by Bruce Langford

I HAVE known Richard Young for twenty-five years. We met as students at a small, conservative Baptist college in Southern California. And while we have not always been in contact over the last quarter of a century, our lives have run a surprisingly parallel course. It's a course your life may have taken as well.

Even before Richard and I met, our lives were very similar. We were both raised in small towns, Richard in the Pacific Northwest, I in the South. We both married our high school sweethearts—an enduring choice for him and a mistake I later corrected. We both were raised with a religiously narrow view of the world—a tradition and a point of origin that will always be a large part of who we are. But contrary to what we were taught, it no longer seems reasonable to assume we have all the answers, or even worse, that we have the only Truth.

My sense is that we are not alone in this feeling. If you have come from a similar background, you may want to explore other metaphors for the Truth as well—especially in a way that does not negate the truth and beauty inherent in Western Christianity.

What brings us all to this point may be that fundamental, orthodox religions seek to solve the inevitable mysteries of life by focusing solely on the externals of fixed idols, absolute ideas, and anthropomorphic images of God: While the picture of the universe this paints is not without a certain degree of comfort, it does require, eventually, that the seeker *look no further.* Inevitably it drops us at the door of "no answer," or at least none we can comprehend. If we want to move beyond blind faith, or worse, resignation, we must look to other approaches, including those present in early Christianity.

The spiritual path of the mystics, which this book expertly explores, offers no easy answers and makes no religious promises. It does not enfold a seeker in the comfort of hard and fast rules. Its focus is inward, subjective, and full of contradictions. It beckons to us from behind a "Cloud of Unknowing" and its secrets are easily diminished when put into words by the discursive intellect. Perhaps that's why its appeal is limited, and why even those who have blazed a trail through the "divine darkness" are reluctant to articulate much beyond "Look! See for yourself!"

Over the last few years, the mystic traditions of the East have made their way into the West, expertly interpreted by writers such as D.T. Suzuki and Alan Watts. But the time has come for those of us raised with the metaphors of traditional Christianity to rediscover our own Gnostic, experiential tradition—a tradition expurgated from the Faith by the early Church. If mainstream Christianity is to survive as anything more than a hollow shell of some former glory, this rediscovery is essential.

Mystic faith is as much psychology as religion. It is less a way of looking into eternity than a way of seeing eternity HERE and NOW. The difference this shift in viewpoint creates is profound. As a psychologist with a religious background, Richard Young shows us the difference that emerges when we live life mindfully in the present moment. He reveals the Truth by being truthful with us. He is honest about his own experience and thus opens the way for us to respond to his call to experience a deeper spirituality in our religious practices and our daily lives.

And that is the crux of the matter: *experience.* While it is the role of science to quantify the truth and the role of religion to explain it, only mystical spirituality invites us to *experience* the

Truth and then return to bring peace to the village. This book serves just that purpose.

Finally, speaking of experience, while the experience of editing this book began as a "ego project," it soon turned into a labor of love. It propelled me onward and inward with each new story. May this time spent with a fellow traveler do the same for you.

BRUCE LANGFORD, Senior Editor
Pathways: A Magazine of Psychological and
Spiritual Transformation
Riverside, California

PREFACE

Call it midlife crisis, depression, alienation, the dark night of the soul, the opening of a new path. But honor it. Listen. Respond. In the beginning all you know is that the old pillars of your identity no longer support the weight of your being. It is time to leave behind the achievements and virtues you have laboriously accumulated during the first part of your life.

SAM KEEN

Would you remain within your tiny kingdom, a sorry king, a bitter ruler of all he surveys, who looks on nothing yet who would still die to defend it? This little self is not your kingdom.

A COURSE IN MIRACLES

IT WAS the spring of 1988 and Southern California was resplendent in sunshine and wildflowers. I was thirty-five years old and had just completed my doctoral degree in psychology after eight years of juggling family, career, and school. I was still married to the same woman and my two sons did not appear to hate me (knock on wood!). While going to graduate school, I had also helped to build one of the most successful psychotherapy clinics in Southern California. My three partners and I employed more than thirty people and maintained five offices in four cities. I was also about to complete my twelfth year as an associate professor of psychology at a small liberal arts college and had just been appointed to chair the department. On top of all of this, my family and I were in the process of moving into our two-story dream house, my wife and I drove expensive German cars, and my first book had just been accepted for publication. I had achieved virtually every personal and professional goal I had ever set for myself.

There was only one small problem: I was not happy. In fact, I was clinically depressed. No one knew this, of course, because I hid the pain beneath a veneer of good humor and professional activity. In other words, I smiled a lot and worked all the time. But whenever I turned my gaze inward, all I could see was emptiness, pretension, and "grasping after wind." The things I had worked so hard and long to achieve no longer seemed worth the effort. I was confused and more than a little frightened. Something was very wrong and I knew it. I had obeyed all the rules, made all the right choices, and fulfilled all my obligations. So why the hell was I in so much pain? I felt betrayed and angry and . . . foolish.

Even now I can't be sure exactly when the depression began. I just know I became acutely aware of it shortly after my doctoral commencement ceremony. My first assumption was that I was simply suffering from "post-goal-attainment letdown." I had worked hard for many years to finish my degree and now I didn't know quite what to do with myself. For a short time I considered pursuing a new goal, medical school, in order to relieve my suffering. I tried to convince myself that by becoming a "real doctor" I would find a renewed sense of meaning and purpose. I went so far as to visit the campus of a local school of osteopathy and to outline the prerequisite science courses I would need to take prior to admission.

My wife, Nancy, was initially quite supportive of this idea. She even went with me to visit the medical school and seemed excited by what she saw there. Then, over a period of several weeks, she began to have serious doubts. I think she had started to enjoy the extra time and energy I now had for her and the boys and did not relish the idea of once more being the wife of a full-time (and compulsive) student. She pointed out that our children had never known a father who was not away at school. Although I argued with her at first, trying to convince her it would be very different this time, I too had begun to question my own motivation and the wisdom of my new plan.

It was starting to dawn on me that my current crisis of meaning went much deeper than I wanted to admit and that medical school would never solve the problem. I realized I could no longer look to external things to fill the void in my heart. No amount of changing and rearranging life, no measure of added effort or increased "doing" would suffice. I had tried these strategies many times through the years and I knew how useless they were. This time the journey would have to be inward. As Alan Watts wrote,

> It is obvious that unless we come face to face with the difficulty in ourselves, everything to which we look for salvation is nothing more than an extra curtain with which to hide that difficulty from our eyes.[1]

Not really knowing how to proceed, I decided to give myself permission to stay miserable for a while instead of trying to medicate my pain away with some kind of activity. I began to "sit down" in the midst of my despair and try to figure things out. This decision was neither bold nor courageous. I just didn't know what else to do.

The past several years have been filled with my often faltering attempts to identify the difficulty in myself. While I am still unsure of how far I have come on this journey, I do know I no longer feel imprisoned by the despair of my limited definition of myself. In fact, I can look back on this particular "dark night of the soul," not with pain or regret, but with a strange feeling of gratitude and appreciation. I see now it was the beginning of my journey towards Home. Of course, one of the many things I learned while I was in the far country is that I never left Home at all. I only dreamed I had.

What follows are insights about my life and experiences that I have been able to gather along the way. They are incomplete (since I'm still breathing) and less than enlightening (since I'm still in love/hate with my ego). But it seems that writing them down has been a requirement for further progress. I wrote this book for myself. Which means, of course, that I wrote it for you.

INTRODUCTION

The story of the prodigal son is such a favorite theme, both for Buddhists and Christians, and in this do we not discover something eternally true, though tragic and unfathomable, which lies so deep in every human heart? Whatever this may be, the will finally succeeds in recognizing itself, in getting back to its original abode. The sense of peace one finds in Enlightenment is indeed that of a wanderer getting safely home.

D. T. SUZUKI

The son has been separated from the father, meaning he has been living a life that's inappropriate to his real heritage. The son is the temporal aspect, and the father is the eternal aspect of the same being. The father represents the natural order from which you have been removed. You are trying to find your character, which you inherit from your father. Atonement is bringing your own personal and contemporary program into accord with the life momentum out of which you have come.

JOSEPH CAMPBELL

LET'S BEGIN with a story about a little boy and his father. It is a true story, although it never actually happened. Or perhaps it did happen and I just don't remember it. But there is always a chance you will remember it, so listen carefully. Either way, it's true.

■

A little boy sat on the large front steps of his house, nervously waiting for his dad to come home from work. It was twilight and a chilly October breeze was blowing leaves across the yard. The old stone steps radiated the winter cold through his denim trousers and made him wish he was inside standing over the gas floor furnace in the hall. But he had to wait. He sat with his pudgy cheeks resting in his hands and stared at the street corner where his dad's big blue car appeared every evening at about this time.

Why did his little sister always have to come in his room and bother his stuff? Sometimes he wished he didn't even have a little sister. Why did she have to be such a brat? He hadn't really hit her that hard, but she went crying to mom anyway. What a baby. If she would have left his room when he told her to, he wouldn't be here now waiting to tell his dad what he had done.

He caught a flash of blue out of the corner of his eye as his dad's car turned onto their street and then pulled slowly into the driveway. He saw his dad wave and smile, but the tightness in his chest and throat kept him from waving back. He watched his father lock the car and move towards him in giant strides across the leaf-cluttered yard.

At that moment, all of the fear and anger that had been building up inside him all day became just too much to bear. With hot tears flowing down his face, he jumped off the steps and started running down the sidewalk. He didn't know where he was going or why, but he knew that he had to run. At first he could hear his father's voice calling out, "Come back here, David, and tell me what's wrong. David, come back."

The little boy ran for what seemed to him like an eternity. When he finally reached the streetlight at the corner, he threw his arms around its stone coldness and cried bitterly. He had never felt so miserable or so alone in his entire young life. He wanted so badly to just disappear so he wouldn't have to face his father.

Then, as if by magic, his father knelt by his side. "What is it, pal? Tell me what's wrong."

At first the words fairly raced out of the little boy's mouth. "Lisa came into my room without permission, and she almost broke my model airplane that you gave me for Christmas, and I tried to make her go and she wouldn't, so I hit her and now mom's mad at me . . ." He stopped suddenly, almost as much for being out of words as for seeing the concern deepen in his father's expression. In that moment, it seemed as if the anger he had so carefully nurtured towards his sister for the past few hours just disappeared as new tears began their long journey towards his chin.

The father looked steadily into his son's eyes and said, "I don't care what happened, David. It's never okay to hit your little sister. It's never okay. Do you understand?"

"Yes daddy, I know, but Lisa . . ."

"No buts. It's never okay."

"I know, daddy. I . . . I'm sorry."

His father picked him up quietly in his strong arms and held him close as he began to walk back toward the house. "I know it's not always easy being the big brother. But you do it pretty well most of the time."

As they walked up the stone steps and passed through the front door into the warmth of the living room, the little boy buried his face in his father's neck. As he breathed deeply of his dad's aftershave, he realized he was glad to be back home.

·

As a psychotherapist, I could explore the ideas about parent-child relationships and the archetypal feelings of returning home that are contained in this story. But then it would lose some of its magic, and the ideas would lose their power. More importantly, you would miss the opportunity to interpret it in the context of your own experience and for the child within you to discover the truths it communicates.

Milton Erickson, the famous hypnotherapist, believed that the greatest teachings are those that reach down into the unconscious mind. Such "unconscious learnings" involve an intuitive understanding of the symbolic meanings and universal/ individual truths and are less concerned with rational thoughts and ideas. When we are moved or inspired by an experience, it is because our unconscious has been touched and changed. Erickson also believed these learnings occur more easily in the natural kind of trance states we experience when we allow ourselves to be carried away by the words of a teacher or a story, a work of art, or a piece of music. At such moments, we surrender ourselves to the experience, becoming something more than just a separate ego in a vast sea of other separate egos, and are transported inward to a place of timelessness, wisdom, and wholeness. In other words, we return Home.

All of the great spiritual teachers and social innovators of history have been master storytellers. Buddha and Christ, Gandhi and Martin Luther King all liked to tell a good story. These were men who knew how to speak in a way that could change a person's heart and mind. There is something almost magical about stories of real people facing real dilemmas as well as parables of imaginary people and events that put us in touch with ourselves and others. Somehow they enable us to integrate unknown or disparate parts of our personalities into a greater unity and to experience our connectedness to other human beings. Besides all that, they make us feel good.

Facts are all well and good, but they are easily forgotten while stories, and the truths they contain, are not. Do you remember your phone number when you were five years old? Probably not. But how about the story of Cinderella or of David and Goliath? Erickson once said that if you want to learn how to become a good therapist or a good teacher, start telling stories to eight-year-olds.

This book is a collection of stories and essays (which are really just stories about stories) I have written over the past several years. Most are factual and autobiographical, although I have thrown in a couple of myths and parables for good measure. But whether factual or mythical, they are all true.

All are stories about a little boy who ran away from home for reasons he can never quite remember. He is a prodigal who left his home in the Eternal Oneness and ventured into the far country of human existence to seek a fortune of experiences. The fortune was never found, but something of infinite value was lost. By entering into this world of dreams and nightmares, he quickly forgot who he was. In the process, he ended up eating slop with the hogs.

Now he has decided he must return to the real world. He must make his way back Home to his Source to rediscover the eternal mystery of his true identity. All he has to guide him in this holy quest is an unshakable desire and the faint sound of his Father's voice.

Each of these stories is a letter to Someone at Home, letting them know I'm on my way and will get there just as soon as I can.

1

EGO PROJECTS

The whole order of things fills me with a sense of anguish, from the gnat to the mysteries of incarnation; all is entirely unintelligible to me, and particularly my own person. Great is my sorrow, without limits. None knows of it, except God in heaven, and He cannot have pity.

SOREN KIERKEGAARD

When the human being developed the power to be aware of himself, to know that he knows—in other words when the cortex was formed over the original brain—he fell from grace. That was the fall of man, because when he felt the sensation of being in charge, of being in control of himself, he became anxious. Am I aware enough of myself? Have I taken enough factors into consideration? Have I done all that should be done? When he asked these questions of himself for the first time, he started to tremble, and this was the fall of man.

ALAN WATTS

WHAT makes us uniquely human is not our opposable thumb, our cerebral cortex, or even our genius for social organization. Dolphins have two of these and monkeys have all three. These qualities are all downstream from the true source of our human nature. The headwaters is that we have evolved to the point where we are conscious of ourselves. We humans are the one creature capable of living life and, at the same time, observing and evaluating ourselves as we live it. We have the unique capacity, due to our cognitive and linguistic ability to represent the world symbolically, to think about OURSELF. In *The Denial of Death*, Ernest Becker writes about this uniquely human ability.

> *Man [sic] has a symbolic identity which brings him sharply out of nature. He is a symbolic self, a creature with a name, a life history. He is a creator with a mind that soars out to speculate about atoms and infinity, who can place himself imaginatively at a point in space and contemplate bemusedly his own planet. This immense expansion, this dexterity, this ethereality, this self-consciousness gives to man literally the status of a small god.*[1]

I don't suppose that dogs or cats or kangaroos spend much time ruminating about themselves or about the meaning and purpose of their lives. Dogs and cats and kangaroos can even look into a pool of water without seeing their own reflection. All they see is water. We human creatures are quite different. When we look into the pool, all we can see is ourselves.

I can still remember one of the first times in my life that I became consciously aware of myself as a distinct and separate individual. I was probably only four years old at the time. We were living in a fourplex apartment near the railroad tracks in Pasco, Washington. I was alone in the bathroom, staring at myself in the full-length mirror that was attached to the back of the door. For some unknown reason, I was scrutinizing every detail of my face. I was especially fascinated with my own eyes because I wanted to see what was behind them. My fantasy was that if I looked hard enough, I would see two little kids looking out at me, one from each eye.

At some point in this little game, I began saying over and over again in my head, "This is my face, this is me!" I felt what I would now identify as a sense of awe and wonder, but there was also a feeling of confusion and disbelief, even fear. It was as if there were another voice, deeper inside and much quieter, saying, "This can't be me, there must be something more." After a while, I ran to our tiny kitchen to find my mother because I was beginning to feel very lonely and afraid.

I am using adult words and concepts to describe a child's intuition. But that intuition insisted that my "face" wasn't really me. If it were, I would have good reason to be frightened. Such an insight is usually reserved for little children, mystics, and the insane.

Throughout history, scientists, philosophers, and poets have celebrated humanity's possession of self-awareness and the reasoning ability that goes with it. It has been heralded as the crowning glory of creation or as the ultimate evolutionary achievement of human nature, depending upon which metaphorical framework you prefer. Who can argue with the creative genius and magnificent "consciousness" of a Michelangelo, a Shakespeare, an Einstein, or a one-year-old taking his or her first steps? We are symbolic creatures who have evolved the cognitive ability to stand above our surroundings and to fashion them, within limits, according to our own desires. We have the power to contemplate eternity. We can even contemplate ourselves. As Becker said, we have "the status of a small god." But small gods must pay a price for their divinity. If self-awareness is our greatest gift, it is also our biggest curse.

The "Fall" into Self-Consciousness

Self-consciousness automatically produces a duality between the self and everything that is not-self. From the moment of our first awareness, we develop the unshakable conviction that we are separate and distinct from all other selves. This is the birth of our separative ego-sense. We live our lives apart—alienated from God, from nature, and from one another—because we accept the evidence of our senses that everything and everyone is essentially *disconnected*. We become blind to our unity within the created order, unable to identify with the higher Self which permeates all forms in existence. Such is our pride and such is our pain.

Every major religion has a cosmology that symbolically describes our "fall" from the direct experience of unity with the Eternal into the distorted perception of a self/other dichotomy that is born of self-consciousness. In Mahayana Buddhism, the source of all suffering is the perception of duality and the refusal to see that consciousness is all that exists. Hinduism equates suffering and limitation with ignorance of the fact that the individual self (*Atman*) is identical with the indwelling, all-pervading Supreme Being (*Brahman*). Judeo-Christian tradition describes this same regression from unity to differentiation in the mythic story of the Garden of Eden: When we ate of the "tree of the knowledge of good and evil," that is, when our self-consciousness led us to distinguish between things (good and evil, self and other, God and creature, etc.), we fell from innocence and were banished from the paradise of self-forgetfulness. It was as though we all looked into the full-length mirror on the back of the bathroom door. We saw our own "nakedness," our own selves, for the first time and were so enchanted and terrified that we have been unable to look away ever since. We have forgotten that the face in the mirror is not really our face at all. It isn't even a good likeness.

To be self-conscious, to possess, nurture, and protect a self that is seen as separate and distinct from all other selves, means to be afraid. Fear is one consequence of knowing the difference between good and evil and between self and other. Anything that is not-self poses a potential threat to the safety and integrity of our island of consciousness. Therefore, we must always be on guard against pain and betrayal. We must be constantly prepared to defend the actions and opinions of our ego at a moment's notice.

In addition to casting us in the role of separate and isolated egos, our self-awareness also makes us believe in the ultimate reality of the body. We come to identify our existence and being with our physical selves. Instead of seeing ourselves as eternal beings who are temporarily riding around in a casing of flesh, we begin to believe we are finite creatures who cannot escape a temporal and spatial body which is subject to illness and death. We forget that life and death are one, that they are just different seasons of the same cycle of existence, and we accept the ego-illusion that death is the end of being. As a result, we become obsessed with our own personal survival and paranoid about the safety and survival of those that we love. The separated, finite ego must be protected at any cost when we accept the idea that this is all we are. Therefore the ego must always triumph no matter who or what must be sacrificed. At the very least, we must move through this world carefully, planning our every action with cunning and stealth, so we won't be diminished or overwhelmed. When our strategies to predict and control life so as to ensure our safety and survival fail, as surely they must, we can become like wounded animals that have been cornered by a savage adversary. At such moments, we are all capable of engaging in monumental evil in our last-gasp efforts to repel the threat of nonbeing and avoid plunging headfirst into the abyss. All of this is enough to make us run to find our mothers in the kitchen.

The Twin Terrors

The fear born of the perception of separateness and the belief that the self is contained only within the body has two variations. First of all, we fear life. More to the point, we are afraid of our smallness and impotence in the face of life. Compared with the vast scope and power of the cosmos, "creation out of the void," we are only "a wisp of smoke that appears for a little time and then is gone." The absolute size and majesty of a transcendent creation stands in frightful contrast to the insignificance of our little, isolated selves. The universe mocks us. Rudolf Otto called this the "*mysterium tremendum et fascinosum*," the feeling of overwhelming fear, fascination, and anguish in the presence of the cosmos.

The second manifestation of our fear is the fear of death. This is our most primal fear, the absolute terror of nonbeing. Death, the ever-present and unavoidable witness to the finitude of the body, is an absolute affront to our conscious ego which identifies itself with that body. Death renders all of the ego's efforts toward meaning and purpose in life absurd. It is ridiculous that we should have a mind that can soar out to contemplate eternity and a body that must inevitably decay and die. In the face of such absurdity, why bother to do anything at all? What profit is there in being god-like in our intellect and abilities, different from all other creatures, when, like them, we will surely return to dust and be forgotten? What kind of god would engineer such a sadistic joke, such elaborate food for worms?

Erich Fromm, the famous psychoanalyst, once made a very interesting point about insanity. He said we should not ask ourselves why some people go crazy. Rather, we should ask why *more* people don't lose their minds given the inescapable dilemmas of human existence. Fromm believed we are able to remain relatively sane throughout our lives only because we distract ourselves by various means from the awareness of our own alienation and impotence. If we were to confront directly the reality of our situation, at least as defined by the ego, it would probably drive a good many of us right out of our minds. He wrote,

> *Considering man's [sic] position in the world, his separateness, aloneness, powerlessness, and his awareness of this, one would expect this burden to be more than he can bear, so that he would, quite literally, "go to pieces" under the strain. Most people avoid this outcome by compensatory mechanisms like the overriding routine of life, conformity with the herd, the search for power, prestige, and money, dependence on idols . . . in short, by becoming crippled. All these compensatory mechanisms can maintain sanity, provided they work, up to a point. The only fundamental solution which truly overcomes potential insanity is the full, productive response to the world which in its highest form is enlightenment.[2]*

Our combined fears of life and death are so powerful and potentially overwhelming that we must find some way to ignore or at least control them in order to undertake self-confident action in the world. Without some method of repression or denial, we would simply be paralyzed by these fears. So we follow the routine with blinders firmly in place, we conform to public opinion, and we search for meaning in life. Or conversely, we behave impulsively and irresponsibly, we rebel against authority, and we embrace nihilism. It doesn't really matter which course we choose since they all accomplish the same unconscious goal: They protect us from seeing the stark picture of reality that has been created by the separated ego. Instead of confronting our sense of isolation and powerlessness, which would eventually lead us to confront the illusions upon which these feelings are based, we go to college to get a degree, to get a better job, to buy a bigger house, to provide for our children, to . . . forget.

The Birth of the Project

The separated ego engages in the frantic process of creating and endlessly refining an identity and a life's work. Through its feverish pursuit of this "project," as John-Paul Sartre called it, the ego is able to distract itself from the fears of life and death it has created through its belief in duality. This "project of separateness" is composed of our character or personality style and our style of life which includes our dreams and goals, our values and beliefs, and our hopes for meaning and fulfillment. Living out the project is a compensatory mechanism enabling us to feel that what we do is somehow meaningful and important while denying the incapacitating perception of our own impotence in the face of uncontrollable Creation. It also helps us avoid the despair of knowing we must one day die.

Ego projects almost always have a compulsive feeling to them. In a sense, the mad pursuit of our projects in an attempt to cope with the twin terrors of life and death *is* our primary addiction. All other forms of addiction (work, alcohol, drugs, sex, etc.) are just expressions or variations of this one. Compulsions (what the Buddha called attachments) have the ability to alter consciousness temporarily, sometimes giving us a glimpse of another state of mind that is less separative.

For example, notice how you feel after the next time you have had to concentrate intently on a problem or task at work for twelve or fourteen hours. When you get home and are soaking luxuriously in the tub, soothing away the aches and pains of the day, see if you don't experience a slightly different state of mind. As you are enveloped in a womb of warm water, notice how hard it is to stay angry at your co-worker who got back late from lunch and didn't even apologize. Watch how the normal worries and concerns of life don't seem quite so pressing, at least for the moment.

Without knowing it or labeling it as such, you are in an altered state of consciousness. This is a state that is less defined by the separation between ourselves and the rest of life and is, therefore, far less painful. To a lesser degree, it is the same state of mind that is the mark and goal of all religious experience and which has been described most eloquently by the mystics of various spiritual traditions throughout history. (I knew it! Soaking in the hot tub *is* just as good as going to church!)

But the glimpse of unitive consciousness that we receive in this way is always temporary. It cannot permanently transform our minds—it will only serve as a painful reminder of what we don't normally experience. And next time, since the human mind quickly accommodates to "mood-altering experiences," I won't experience the same "relief" unless I up the dose and work for *fifteen* hours.

Projects also come in an infinite variety of shapes and sizes. There are probably as many different projects as there are people in the world, so an exhaustive taxonomy is quite impossible. For someone who is a workaholic, the project may involve the gradual development of a Type A personality combined with the single-minded pursuit of power, money, and success— in the sincere belief that these things will transform consciousness (our most secret hope) and give life meaning and purpose. For someone else, the project might consist of bearing children and creating a family legacy—in the secret hope that this will purchase some degree of immortality. The variations and complexities of projects are endless. In addition, projects are not static but will evolve slowly and sometimes change cataclysmically throughout the life cycle.

On the individual level, projects are judged effective if they enable us to repress our fears of life and death while providing our lives with apparent meaning and direction. But projects must also interface with the cultural norms and expectations of the world that we inhabit. They combine the influences of individual need and sociocultural expectation, then mediate between these frequently conflicting forces. When our project is grossly inconsistent with the norms and standards of our particular society or group, for example, it may still be quite effective in meeting our existential needs to repress the fear of life and death. But we will probably find ourselves labeled as strange, sick, bad, or crazy.

The best projects not only meet our existential needs to repress fear and create meaning but are also relatively consistent with the major values and expectations of our current society and culture. In other words, some degree of conformity is necessary to mental health. The one exception to this principle occurs when people who possess similar variations in their projects band together in order to force society to change enough to make room for those variations (e.g., feminism, gay rights).

When Projects Fail

On the surface, projects would seem to be a fairly good trade off. They do narrow and distort our perception of the world and of ourselves, thereby limiting our vision of truth and reality. But they also enable us to fulfill our existential needs for meaning and purpose and provide us with the means to pursue our goals and live productively. Projects also serve to distract us from the absurdity of our finite existence and the tremendous despair that results from tacitly understanding our condition of impotence in relation to the cosmos. They would seem to be the best approach to life that the separative ego can possibly design.

There is only one problem. Sooner or later, outward circumstances or our own actions will force us to recognize that we cannot control life. The ego's attempt to control reality through the compulsive pursuit of a project is a bit like a fish trying to balance the ocean on its head. The best it can do is to sincerely believe that it is succeeding. It swims around very slowly and carefully each day in a tight little circle, feeling rather unappreciated by the other fish who do not seem to understand the arduous task it has undertaken on their behalf. The fish is most careful not to leave the security of its little circle for fear the ocean will slip and fall off the top of its head. Of course, this poor misunderstood fish dies of an anxiety related disorder at a rather young age, without ever having felt the tremendous peace of knowing that the ocean has always been balancing him.

There is one other thing that tends to undermine our project. No matter what we do or how we live, we shall surely die; and we cannot avoid this knowledge forever. Projects always fail to rescue us from an eventual confrontation with our own mortality. When this happens, all the previously repressed terrors of life and death storm back into our consciousness, and the project begins to disintegrate.

Project decompensation leads us inevitably to a state of existential despair, wherein we are forced to consciously confront our long-ignored fears. We are never more fragile or more prone to serious emotional disturbance than at these moments in our lives. All our comfortable props are knocked out from under us, and we feel totally alone in the universe.

There is usually a deep sense of futility and loss of hope as we face our powerlessness to change or control our lives. We become confused, disoriented, and unable to make the simplest decisions for fear we will make our situation worse. We may believe God is punishing us for some unpardonable sin we cannot recall or that He has simply abandoned us to our pain because He has better things to do. Our bodies may betray us as we succumb to physical illness or struggle vainly to overcome our pervasive lethargy and loss of motivation. Despair may well be the most frightening and painful condition a human being can experience. It is little wonder Kierkegaard called it "the sickness unto death."

It is not a pretty sight to watch someone whose project is beginning to fail. It is even less fun when that failing project happens to be your own. I know because my shining jewel of a project, "my precious" as Golum in *The Lord of the Rings* would call it, began its death-throes several years ago. I tried everything I could think to do: more work, more education, more accomplishment, more church responsibilities, more power and influence, more sex, more cigarettes (sometimes after sex). Nothing worked. My life became completely unmanageable. I was out of control. Then I began to realize that my project was in a fairly rapid decline. I started to see it as nothing more than my ego's empty promise of power, immortality, and transformation. It was a pervasive lie dressed up in decent clothes so it would be presentable in church.

Awakening to Oneness

What are the options when our project begins to fail? The first line of defense is usually to refine it and then to invest more energy trying to make it work. So we go into therapy and decide to worry less about our finances, avoid power struggles with our colleagues at work, and spend more quality time with the family. Voila! A "new, improved" project.

But what if the improvements don't work? And they won't for long. Then we may have to go back to the ego drawing board and design an entirely new project (like going to medical school, getting a divorce, or buying a new sports car). While such radical changes in our character and lifestyle may feel like rebirth for a time, they are really just expensive ways to prolong the inevitable. Sooner or later we will come full-circle back to despair because that's what projects do—they ultimately *create* despair.

Do we really have to settle for a rigid, neurotic existence, full of pain and devoid of any lasting peace, in order to avoid psychosis? What kind of a deal is that? And what of Fromm's suggestion that we all learn to abandon our fears and escape into enlightenment? I have this great fantasy of standing on a street corner in utter despair, waiting to throw myself in front of the first beer truck that comes along. All of a sudden, Erich Fromm runs up to me, grabs my arm, and frantically shouts, "Don't do it, there's another way! You can seek enlightenment!" I turn slowly and look at him with tears of joy and gratitude in my eyes and say, "Ah . . . what's enlightenment?"

There are problems with this option as well. Even though awakening or enlightenment has been recommended by mystics of both East and West for centuries, there are very few people in any given generation who really understand what it is and what it requires in terms of spiritual discipline. Fewer still ever experience it. But there is an even more frustrating complication. Any Zen master or Christian contemplative worth his or her incense will tell you that the earnest desire to understand and experience *satori* or *kensho* or salvation or whatever you want to call it (a rose by any other name) is the very reason we don't experience it.

Now let me see if I've got this right. If I don't know about enlightenment, I will be stuck in the endless twistings and turnings of my ego project. But if I search for it diligently, living a moral life and practicing the various spiritual disciplines with dedication and vigor, then it will elude me forever. Terrific. Apparently, in the game of spiritual attainment, to seek after anything is to remain fixated in the dualistic illusion that I (who am essentially divine) could possibly lack something. Since it is this self-other dualism that is the original crux of the problem, I do not get to pass Go and I do not collect my $200. All of this is enough to send my ego screaming into the night.

But wait, there's more. Those few individuals who have been able to negotiate the rapids of spiritual life and achieve some degree of illumination seem to be unable to describe their experience in plain English (or plain Chinese). In other words, they have no words. They rely heavily on the use of paradox, parables, poetry, and stories to express the essence of their wisdom. As Mu-mon, the thirteenth century Chinese master wrote,

> *Words cannot describe everything.*
> *The heart's message cannot be delivered*
> *in words.*
> *If one receives words literally, he will be lost.*
> *If he tries to explain with words, he will not*
> *attain enlightenment in this life.*[3]

Even though enlightenment is considered by many to be the culmination of humanity's deepest desire and need, it remains shrouded in mystery and misunderstanding. And from what I have read, it isn't easy either. In fact, most of us would never even consider the difficult path of pursuing salvation when our project is doing well. Why fix it if it ain't broke? If we happen to be blessed/cursed with a fairly productive and satisfying project, we may stay stuck for years in our illusions of competence and control. But with any luck at all, we will fail. Herein lies the secret wisdom of pain. Project decompensation opens a door on Reality that may lead us to the insight we need to finally abandon our fears of life and death and the endless rounds of suffering they inflict.

I can finally say with some degree of honesty that I am glad my project was doomed to failure. Thank God my natural narcissism and overblown self-confidence led me to make just enough mistakes along the way that the ocean finally slid off my head. And thank God for the inescapable fact of our bodily death which serves to remind us, while we are yet alive, that we have been deceiving ourselves.

When we looked into the mirror of self-awareness, we mistook our reflection for our real Self. Ever since then, we have lived in a nightmare of painful isolation because we really believe we are nothing but an ego with a body. So we spend our lives longing for Something we can never name. But help is on the way, even though it doesn't feel much like help at first.

The death of our project is the occasion of our liberation. It is precisely when our project begins to fail, when our pain and despair are most intense, that we are given the opportunity to abandon our fascination with the separated and terrified ego and surrender to the Oneness that is our true reality.

In such moments, we can begin to awaken from our nightmare of separation and discover our unity with all Being. As Wes Nisker once wrote about the "crazy wisdom" inherent in enlightened Mind,

> *Crazy wisdom sees that we live in a world of many illusions, that the Emperor has no clothes, and that much of human belief and behavior is ritualized nonsense. Crazy wisdom understands antimatter and old Sufi poetry; loves paradox and puns and pie fights and laughing at politicians. Crazy wisdom flips the world upside down and backward until everything becomes perfectly clear.*[4]

At some point in the journey, we must find the courage to face our terrors of life and death and transcend the limitations of our ego project. We must dare to flip the world upside down and backward to finally make sense of our lives.

MEDITATION: *Dealing with Fear*

There are many situations and experiences in our lives that are capable of arousing fear and anxiety within us. When we try to design a strategy (ego project) to get in control of these fears or when we work to exclude them from consciousness (mindlessness), we only succeed in worsening our plight. The following meditation, based on Buddhist *mindfulness* techniques which are thousands of years old, may help you deal more effectively with fear when it arises.

Find a quiet room and a comfortable chair. Sit down easily, close your eyes, and relax for a few moments. Just let your body settle into the chair and try to clear your mind of the concerns of the day. Focus on the in-and-out sensation of your breath passing through your nostrils until you can feel your body relaxing more deeply.

Once you feel fairly calm and relaxed, call to mind a current situation that is causing you a *moderate* degree of anxiety or concern. It could be a presentation you have to give at work or an unresolved argument with your spouse. Whatever the problem, try to recreate it right now in your imagination. Who are the other people involved? What are they saying or doing that provokes your anxiety? What are you being expected to do that is difficult or unpleasant? Visualize the details as if it were happening in this moment. Hold this image in your mind.

Next, gently shift the focus of your attention to your body. Be aware of how the fear or discomfort of this situation expresses itself in your physical being. Where do you feel it? In your chest? In your stomach? Don't try to make the physical or emotional feelings go away and don't get up. Sit with these feelings for a few moments, no matter how intense they seem to become. Invite them into your experience as you would an old friend. Now, let go of the label "fear," and just notice the sensations that are arising in your body. Don't name them, just be aware of them. Do they move? How long do they last? How are these sensations different when you don't label them as fear? What happens as they pass away? Are they replaced by something else?

Finally, repeat the following statement *slowly* in your

mind about twenty times while you focus once more on the sensations of the breath as it passes through your nostrils:

**There Is No Fear in Love;
Perfect Love Casts Out Fear.**

What do you feel in your body now? What sensations are you aware of? What has become of the fear?

Once you have practiced this meditation a few times, you can begin to use this thought as a sort of mantra anytime you are feeling anxious or afraid. Simply repeat the words slowly in your mind as you focus on the rhythm of your breathing.

■

2

DEALING WITH PAIN

But he who loves God has no need of tears, no need of admiration, in his love he forgets his suffering, yea, so completely has he forgotten it that afterwards there would not even be the least inkling of his pain if God Himself did not recall it, for God sees in secret and knows the distress and counts the tears and forgets nothing.

SOREN KIERKEGAARD

Hidden under its miseries, life keeps incredible happiness waiting for one who will search and work for it.

PAUL BRUNTON

IF WE BUILD and defend our ego project because we are trying to deal with our fear of pain and death, then learning to confront and deal with this universal terror might lead us to greater spiritual freedom. Perhaps this is why it is traditional for young Buddhist monks to be taken to a cemetery late at night to meditate on death and decay. My own confrontation with death began several years ago, quite unbeknownst to me, after the birth of our second child.

Suffer the Little Children

From the very start, Adam did things in his own inimitable style. Sometime during the last trimester of pregnancy, our obstetrician told us our unborn child was a "footling breach."

Instead of riding upside down in the womb with his head near the birth canal like most babies, Adam had his head up under his mother's rib cage with just his toes barely dangling near the cervix. It was as though he intended to stick his big toe out into the world first to see how he liked it.

Our doctor went on the explain that this could make labor and delivery more difficult unless he was able to turn the child around just prior to birth. He also said there was a slightly higher risk that the baby could get tangled in the umbilical cord during labor and delivery. After the three of us discussed the pros and cons of various options, the doctor manipulated Nancy's stomach and succeeded in turning Adam upside down. It couldn't have been more than two minutes later when Adam flipped back around like a cork shooting out of a bottle of champagne. Apparently this kid knew how he wanted to come into the world. He wanted to land on his feet.

Adam's first year of life was difficult. It seemed as soon as Nancy weaned him, he began to suffer from terrible stomach cramps and diarrhea after almost every meal. In addition, he seemed to experience chronic cold symptoms and bronchitis. We tried every kind of formula and baby food known to mothers and Gerber's, but nothing helped his digestive problems. We must have taken him to the doctor twenty times, but no one could figure out what was wrong.

As Adam neared his first birthday, Nancy happened to see a public service announcement on television featuring Burt Reynolds and Sally Struthers. They were talking about a rare genetic disorder called Cystic Fibrosis, and they said one of the ways to screen for it with your child is to see if their skin tastes salty whenever you kiss them. Nancy had often commented to me about how salty Adam tasted. I had never given it much thought.

That night when I returned from work, she told me about what she had seen on television. At this point, I had never heard of CF and so I tried to calm her fears. But she insisted we take Adam to be tested. I agreed somewhat reluctantly.

The next day was Saturday, but we went to the clinic anyway and paid the extra fee to see the doctor on call. He was not Adam's regular pediatrician but a fairly young doctor fresh from his residency at U.C.L.A. We told him of our concerns, and he very carefully examined Adam. When he was finished, he tried to assure us that he saw no signs of CF in our son. He went on to say that even though it is a relatively rare disease, he had seen many CF children during his training. But just to be absolutely sure, he referred us to the Cystic Fibrosis Clinic at San Bernardino County Hospital (which we would learn later is one of the best in the country) so Adam could be thoroughly tested. We left his office that day feeling somewhat reassured but still uneasy.

Several weeks later we were able to set up the test and our first appointment with the specialist. By that time, Nancy and I had convinced ourselves this couldn't possibly be Adam's problem. From all we had read about the disease, he was just too vital and energetic to have a terminal illness that robs children of their strength.

I will never forget the day we went to the specialist to hear the results of the tests. We sat in his tiny office, looking at the clown pictures on the walls, while he told us our baby boy had an incurable, genetic disease that would surely cut his life very short. When I heard those horrible words, "The tests are positive," I felt a terrible coldness and rage growing deep within my soul and overflowing into every nerve ending in my body. I remember feeling furious at the doctor for his calm, factual explanation of the diagnosis and treatment. Didn't he realize this was my son upon whom he had just pronounced sentence? I understand now his approach was really the kindest.

In the days that followed, my reaction was one of shock and denial. The doctor couldn't have been talking about my Adam. Maybe the lab technician did the sweat test incorrectly or accidentally switched the results with those of another child. And what about this doctor? Maybe he wasn't the expert everyone said, and we should seek a second or even a third opinion. There must be some mistake!

Eventually the reality of the situation began to sink in and undermine my denial system. Every time I heard my son's deep, rattling cough I could feel the ache deep inside, like a cancer in the marrow of my bones. The pain seemed to wrap itself around my heart like a giant, evil hand that threatened to squeeze all of the joy from my life. There was absolutely nothing I could do to force that hand to release its grip. When I played with him on the floor or held him in my arms, the pain would return: dark, cold, and merciless. I prayed—no, I begged God to heal him and make him whole but there was no answer, at least none I could discern.

Then, without really knowing what I was doing, I started to "take control" of my pain. I began to withdraw from my son and leave him more and more in the care of his mother. I didn't hold him or play with him as much. I tried not to hear his crying in the night or his coughing during the day. I worked more at the practice and the college. And I began to slide into a deep depression I could neither control nor fully understand. I wanted nothing more than to insulate myself from the pain. It was as if I were saying to this precious, innocent child, "Stay away, I can't let you hurt me anymore."

One day, about six months later, I was sitting in my therapy office listening to a mother lament about her eight-year-old son's problems in school. She told me he would do his homework and then refuse to turn it in. He would fight on the playground and then lie about his involvement. He was constantly being held after school for disruptive classroom behavior. This mother had tried everything she could think of to do. She had been working closely with the teacher and principal and had even volunteered to work in her son's classroom two days a week to see if that would help. None of this had been easy for her as she was a single mother and had other children at home. Listening to this woman tell her story, I could hear the hurt and anger in her voice. But I could also hear love and a stubborn commitment to help her son through these problems no matter what the cost.

Driving home that evening I remembered her voice. Somehow it spoke to me of how I had been trying to isolate and protect myself from my own son. And I saw, with the absolute clarity that comes in such moments, the tremendous emotional damage this would cause for both of us. When I arrived home, I walked in the door without a word and took Adam into my arms. I held his soft cheek next to mine and smelled the baby lotion on his skin. And for the first time since he had been diagnosed, I wept.

Adam is sixteen years old now and as full of life and energy as ever. The doctors say he is doing remarkably well, and he has to see the specialist only three or four times a year instead of every month. I know he is being sustained by love and grace. But then, I suppose we all are whether we realize it or not. He is a sophomore in high school this year and a "straight A" student. He takes twenty hours of dance and gymnastic lessons each week and dreams of becoming the next Baryshnikov. He also loves to torment his remarkably patient older brother. I do not know what the future holds for Adam or how much time God will grant him. I do know I will be a part of all of it.

The Secret Blessing of Pain

The first of the Four Noble Truths that the Buddha taught his disciples after his enlightenment is that life is characterized by *duhkha*, usually translated as "pain" or "suffering." He meant that all of our experience is permeated with an overwhelming sense of tension, frustration, and irritation. Suffering is the central problem of human existence. As the Buddha taught:

> *What now is the noble truth of suffering? Birth is suffering; decay is suffering; death is suffering; sorrow, lamentation, pain, grief, and despair are suffering; not to get what one wants is suffering; in short, the five aggregates of clinging are suffering.*[1]

In addition, none of us escapes life completely unscathed. We are all wounded in one way or another, some of us mortally. Even the most stoic among us has cried out in anger and confusion to what seemed like an empty heaven, demanding an explanation. Yet no answer would be sufficient to reduce our sense of outrage at the seeming injustice of pain. It is so manifestly unearned, so completely senseless, and it seems to thrust us further towards the inescapable void of nonbeing and death.

It is in our moments of greatest suffering that we feel most completely alone. Even Jesus cried out on the cross, "My God, why have you forsaken me?" Thomas Merton, the well-known Trappist monk, put it most eloquently when he said,

> *When a man suffers, he is most alone. Therefore, it is in suffering that we are most tested as persons. How can we face the awful interior questioning? What shall we answer when we come to be examined by pain?* [2]

In times of pain and sorrow, we may struggle to tell others the awful reality of our suffering. But mere words often fail to adequately express the fear and emptiness that usually accompany pain. Like Job, we find the sympathies of our friends and family to be trite and sometimes even cruel. We feel forsaken and alone even when surrounded by others who want to help. Despite its universality, pain is a very private experience. It threatens to destroy all our carefully constructed defenses and propel us towards nothingness. Yet it is in that nothingness we find so terrifying that we will finally meet God.

The first and most natural human response to pain and the fear it creates is to try to get our lives and the lives of those we love under some kind of control. We narrow the scope of our existence down into bite-size chunks. We settle for less and less life, exchanging our freedom for compulsion, and then try to talk ourselves into believing we are truly living life to the fullest with only a minimum of risks. We place ourselves in a prison of predictable illusions and feel safer for a while, until life deals us another blow. Then we reduce our liberty and our vision of reality even further.

This strategy for dealing with pain in the present and potential pain in the future makes perfect logical sense.

Unfortunately it doesn't work. In fact, it makes matters worse. As Sam Keen writes,

> *The dominant problem of the human personality is our compulsion to control. We live by compulsions, to have power, to control, to make the world coherent and safe. This, then, is the problem, not the answer.*[3]

The consequence of dealing with our fears of life and death by trying to take control is the same for all of us: increased anxiety, insecurity, worry, depression, and finally despair. This is the price that all non-omnipotent and non-omniscient gods must pay.

What shall we do then when our strategies to control life, to somehow contain it in our hands, succeed only in heaping more coals of fire upon our heads? The all too common answer is to run from it in one way or another. We may try to cover our pain over with various activities, attitudes, and prejudices. We may attempt to dull it with drugs, alcohol, cigarettes, food, sex, or any other of the ten thousand addictions and attachments available to us. We may put up walls between ourselves and other people's pain so we don't have to bear the burden of theirs as well. We can become cynical. And when all else fails, we can blame our fear and pain on someone else. But I know for certain we can never run fast enough or far enough to escape pain. We can only run in a circle that brings us back to pain over and over again until it becomes our constant companion.

Somehow we have to learn to do the opposite of what instinct suggests when we are in pain. We must find the courage to lower our heads and move into the center of our suffering. It is in that forward movement that all of our illusions of being a separate and autonomous ego begin to melt away. Pain is not just a pain, although it is certainly that. It is also a messenger, a bringer of revelation and blessing. Like Jacob, we must be willing to wrestle with the angel of pain all night long, if necessary, to demand our blessing. Even if it ends up putting our hip out of joint, when the struggle is finally over, we will say along with him, "I have seen God face to face and I have lived."

The Word of blessing that the angel of pain speaks to us, when we stop running long enough to hear it, is that we are not alone and never have been. Only egos can be separate, alone, and in pain. The higher Self, from which we all derive our being, is one and eternal. It is an ego illusion that we are living life and are therefore responsible to control it. Life, God, Being is living us. It is all around and within us. It is so close that we miss it. As someone once said, "I don't know who discovered water but I know it wasn't a fish."

Life that is spoken into existence by God's exuberant desire for Self-expression and Self-conscious experience bears us up on every side. We are literally swimming in life and grace. If we insist on always swimming upstream in order to assert the illusion of ego, we will become absolutely exhausted and we will hurt. But if we abandon ourselves to the gentle yet powerful movements of the Divine Current, regardless of where it may take us, then we will find peace.

I had a dream not long ago that I remember quite vividly. I was at the beach on a bright summer day, standing chest-deep in the surf. I was thoroughly enjoying the wonderful sensations of warm sun and cool water, the smell of salt in the breeze, and the sight of sunlight dancing on the ripples. I happened to glance out to sea and noticed a big wave beginning to build. I didn't think much about it at first; but as it got closer, I could see it was growing larger and larger.

My first instinct was to run towards shore, and I actually took a couple of steps in that direction. Then something inside told me to stop. I visualized the wave breaking on top of my head as I tried to outrun it, driving me mercilessly to the bottom. So I turned and faced the wave with great fear in my heart. In the endless moment just before it reached me, towering above like a churning avalanche, I knew I was going to drown.

I took the deepest breath I could, closed my eyes, and dove into the wave. With tremendous force, it pushed me towards the bottom and held me there. I could feel the air being squeezed from my lungs by the sheer weight of the tons of water passing over me. All my puny efforts to swim towards the surface were futile. Just when I was sure that my lungs would burst, I bobbed up on the other side of the wave. As I turned and watched it crashing towards the shore, I saw that after running its course, it slowly dissolved into the sand.

Exhausted and weak, I began walking back towards shore. I looked up to see Adam, standing at the edge of the water and waiting for me. He was smiling, showing me a seashell he had just found. I suddenly noticed how good the warm sun felt on my wet shoulders.

MEDITATION: *Healing the Pain*

Sit comfortably and quietly in a restful place. Take a deep breath through your nose, hold it for a few seconds, and then blow it out through your mouth. Make sure to let all the air out of your lungs. Take another deep breath and repeat the process. Now breathe normally and let your attention stay with the breath. Try to let go of regretful or nostalgic thoughts of yesterday as well as anxious or hopeful thoughts of tomorrow. Stay in the moment by focusing on the rhythm of your breathing.

Gently shift the focus of your awareness to your body. Notice the places in your body where there is discomfort or pain; places that need your loving and healing attention. Don't ignore or resist the pain, whatever or wherever it may be. Don't run from the wave. Be willing to be wounded again, if that is what is necessary for your healing. Now, focus on a particular area and imagine yourself *moving into* the pain—slowly, gently, courageously. Dive into the wave. Be aware of the individual sensations that arise and pass away as you imagine yourself "swimming" through the pain. Feel the burning or aching sensation here, the throbbing over there. Notice how many different sensations make up the experience we call pain. As you continue to journey through these sensations, notice the "distance" that begins to open up between them. Let this spaciousness begin to fill your heart and mind with complete stillness and deep peace.

Place your hand over the part of your body that most needs to be touched and healed. Feel the warmth and pressure of your hand as it begins to send healing energy to the deepest parts of your pain. Now imagine that it is the hand of the divine being from your religious tradition who inspires your greatest love and devotion. It is no longer your hand that gently and lovingly caresses the pain. It is the wonderful hand of Christ or Buddha or the Virgin Mary. Feel the warm, golden light that flows from their hand into your body and then down into the very center of your being. Experience the love and healing in their divine touch. Open your heart to their wisdom and compassion.

As you rise to leave, do so with a prayer of thanksgiving for the healing you have received. Return to this meditation often—there are no limits on Grace.

■

3

CELEBRATE LIFE!

I, God, am your playmate!
I will lead the child in you in wonderful ways
For I have chosen you.
Beloved child, come swiftly to Me
For I am truly in you.

MECHTILD OF MAGDEBURG

I can imagine that someday we will regard our children not as
creatures to manipulate or to change but rather as messengers
from a world we once deeply knew, but which we have long
since forgotten, who can reveal to us more about the true secrets
of life, than our parents were ever able to do.

ALICE MILLER

WHEN I wrote the preceding chapter, I did not intend for Adam to read it at this point in his life because of its discussion of the terminal nature of his disease. Nancy and I had always been as open and honest with him about Cystic Fibrosis as we could be, given his developing level of understanding and maturity. But we had not yet explained to him the facts about the progressive damage being done to his body or about the average lifespan of most CF children. I had often tried to rehearse this future conversation in my head, but I dreaded the day when I would have to tell Adam about these things. As fate or God would have it, he ran across a copy of the chapter in my office and read it.

As you might imagine, this produced a crisis in our family for some time. Nancy and I used this unexpected situation to help Adam understand and begin to accept some of the more frightening eventualities of his illness. We also tried to reassure him as best we could about the remarkable scientific progress that has been made in recent years in the search for a cure for CF.

Children have a remarkable ability to heal themselves of emotional pain if we help them a little. Shortly after the dust settled from this episode, Adam decided to write a paper to express his feelings about CF. I am certain this was his attempt to gain a greater sense of acceptance over something very frightening in his life. I am also certain this is his way of teaching me about life and truth, even though he doesn't know it yet.

Adam asked me if I would be willing to put his writing in a book someday so perhaps other CF children and their families could benefit from it. I agreed.

A Song of Hope

My name is Adam Young, and I am a victim of a rare genetic disease called Cystic Fibrosis. I've had it for twelve years now. Before I tell you my story, let me give you a little information about this disease.

Cystic Fibrosis is passed from parent to child by what are called recessive genes. Two of these recessive genes have to connect in order for a child to "catch" Cystic Fibrosis; one gene from the mother and one gene from the father. CF causes the child's body to make this sticky mucus that coats everything inside like the lungs and digestive system. This makes it hard to breathe sometimes and very hard to digest food. It often causes stomachaches and attracts sicknesses easily.

Anyway, on with my story. I quite often get these terrible, gut-wrenching stomachaches. When I get these throbbing pains, I can hardly think straight. I rapidly perspire as tears fill my eyes. It's as if all my thought and concentration is drained out of me as I feel this horrifying pain. And then, as my stomach pain slowly drifts away, I can begin to start functioning again.

For some reason, my parents can always tell when I start to feel these bad aches coming even before I say anything. This is the time when my dad starts jetting through the house for my medicine while my mom comforts me. After a few minutes of being held, I can feel my enzymes start kicking in, and I start getting a feeling of relief. I can actually feel my enzymes fighting inside of me. It's as if there is a battle taking place inside my stomach as my medicine quickly demolishes the enemy. In case you are wondering, enzymes are the capsules I take so I can digest my food. They are called Pancrease MT 16. They are very powerful, which makes me feel good since my life depends on them.

It's a real, real big drag though because I have to swallow five enzymes after every meal that I eat in order to digest my food. I have to take three after snacks. It's not as bad as it used to be because it used to take me longer to swallow my pills because I was still learning. I remember the day I learned to swallow pills. I was eating dinner at the Cask 'n Cleaver, and I was so happy that I told the waiter about how I was able to take my capsules. I think I was about five years old at the time.

When I go to school, I have to take my medicine at the school office after lunch. I get really tired of it because right after lunch everybody goes out on the playground while I have to go to the office first. But it's not all bad. My friends really make me feel comfortable about my Cystic Fibrosis. If I ever have to do something that concerns my disease, they always understand. So that makes me feel real good. I have no problem talking to my friends about it. I am also surprised by the amount of interest my friends have in Cystic Fibrosis.

The only thing that bugs me is the way some of the kids at school say "Cystic Fibrosis." They don't even try to pronounce it, which I can understand. But instead they say those two strong words, "The Disease." It's not exactly that it bothers me that I have a disease. In fact, the word "disease" doesn't even bother me. It's just that they all say it in a certain way with a certain tone of voice. Sometimes that can just send chills down my spine. But I guess I shouldn't be offended.

When I was in the fifth grade, I did an oral report on Cystic Fibrosis in front of the class. That really scared me. I didn't know if maybe after my report, people and kids would look at me and see me in a different way. That frightened me. My mom came and everything seemed to go well. I received a lot of questions and the class seemed to have a great deal of interest. This made me feel much better. After the report was finished, I noticed that no one seemed to be looking at me or seeing me in a different way even though they knew about the CF. This made me feel great!

None of this would have happened if it was not for my fifth-grade teacher. She showed the most interest out of all of the people at school. Her name was Mrs. Ferrone. She was a great teacher with a loving heart. But something very tragic happened to her last summer. She was killed in a car accident. I was so sad and so devastated when this happened. And I still think about her every day. But not just about her death. I think about what she taught me.

That year Mrs. Ferrone let me open up and share what I had been hiding. That was greater than anything. She helped me to feel so open and so confident in myself. And she taught me that no matter who you are or what you look like, it's what is inside of you that makes a difference.

I know that she can read this paper and that she is listening. So I just want her to know that I will never, ever forget her.

4

BIRDSONG

Of sorrow he knew nothing, unless it was the birdsong above him; for the sweetness of it pierced his heart and made his little bosom swell. His nature and his yearning so compelled him.
WOLFRAM VON ESCHENBACH

When the wild bird cries its
Melody from the treetops,
Its voice carries the message
Of the Patriarch.
When the mountain flowers are in bloom,
Their full meaning comes with their scent.

ZEN POEM

THIS CHAPTER and the next are about birds. No, I'm not an ornithologist, and I don't keep birds as pets. I'm not even particularly fond of birds, although I imagine our three cats probably like them. But I have learned some important truths about the journey Home from my encounters with a couple of common, garden-variety birds. So before the nurse comes with my evening medication, let me tell you a story about a young sparrow whose voice changed my view of life.

When I was six years old, my father bought my first BB gun. It was the most inexpensive model that Daisy made at the time, but I was as proud of that rifle as if it had cost a fortune. I can remember Dad taking me out into the fields near our house and teaching me how to shoot in proper military style. He showed me how to hold the rifle butt snugly to my shoulder, where to place my right cheek on the stock, and how to line up the two sights along the barrel. He also took great care to explain to me the rules of gun safety, such as never pointing a gun at another person even if you "knew" that it was empty, never shooting near or towards houses, and always carrying the gun with the barrel pointed towards the ground.

I took in all this information very solemnly and pledged to my father I would never forget the rules and would always obey them. And I meant it, too. Right up until the time I shot my cousin Penny in the leg because I thought the gun was empty. When I could finally sit down again without help, I swore to myself that I would not play fast and loose with the rules of life ever again. Okay, so I lied.

By the time I was twelve, I had a better and much more expensive Daisy BB gun. It wasn't any more powerful than my first gun, but it was much more accurate. There were several other boys about my age in the neighborhood where I lived who also had BB guns. From time to time, usually on a Saturday morning, we would all get up early and go "hunting." Now our brand of hunting consisted of hiking to a large grove of trees about two miles from my house and shooting birds. The game was to see who could shoot the most sparrows, robins, and starlings in a specified period of time.

One of the boys in our group was named Randy, and we had been best friends since the second grade. We were always fiercely competitive with one another in everything we did. Walking to school together, one of us would usually challenge the other to a foot race. When we played sandlot baseball, we would almost always end up as captains of the opposing teams. Randy was a skinny kid who had moved to our town from Texas. He was very athletic and always gave me a run for my money. He also had a funny accent.

I mention Randy because the kid was a crack shot with a BB

gun. It seemed like he always won the hunting competition and it made me furious. I can only remember winning on one occasion when I killed thirteen birds in two hours and he only got ten. I lined up all thirteen of my "kills" in a row on the ground and looked them over proudly as Randy grudgingly admitted my victory and vowed to beat me next time. It felt great to rout him so thoroughly in his best sport. Then, as we turned towards home to eat lunch, I got the dismal feeling inside that I should bury those dead birds instead of just leaving them on the ground to rot. But I kept on walking without looking back. I didn't want Randy to think I was weak.

On another such hunting expedition, Randy and I were running neck and neck with six confirmed kills each. I also had one probable, but since we couldn't find the body in the bushes, it didn't count. I was stalking a particularly elusive brown sparrow that kept flitting from tree to tree. I could tell it was a female because it lacked the distinctive black markings on its head and chest that always adorn male sparrows. This bird was very smart. Just about the time I would draw a bead on it, the crazy thing would jump to another branch or fly to the next tree. It seemed to stay just out of sight behind leaves and branches no matter what angle I used to approach it. I would see a flash of wing one moment and the twitch of a tail feather the next, but I could never seem to get a clear shot.

I suppose I could have given up and looked for another target, but shooting this particular bird had become a matter of pride. I stopped pursuing for a moment and stood perfectly still. I even slowed the rhythm of my breathing so the sparrow would think I had gone. I remember pretending I was blending into my surroundings—that I was just another part of the landscape. The bird flitted once or twice and then started to settle down. It flew to a relatively low branch that was completely exposed to my line of sight. Then it ruffled up its feathers and sat there motionless in the bright morning sun. Now I could kill her because she didn't even know I was there. Her death would attest to my skill and assure my victory over Randy once more.

I quietly brought my BB gun into position, being careful not to rattle the BB's in the barrel, and stared at the sparrow along the sights. For some reason, I noticed she looked very pretty as the morning sun shown on her brown feathers. I saw the gentle yellow tinting along the edge of her beak, signifying she was still a young bird not long from the nest. I hesitated in taking the shot. Something was wrong. I wanted to kill her so I could win the game. But the thought of watching her drop to the ground made me feel uneasy. At first I was confused. Then I got angry. Why should I care about killing this particular sparrow? I had slain dozens of birds in the past without a second thought. Why was I hesitating now? The more I became aware of my feeling of shame, the angrier I got at her. Now she had to die. I lined up the sights once more and quickly took the shot. My anxiety caused me to pull the trigger too hard, jerking the barrel of the gun off line. I was able to catch a glimpse of the BB as it narrowly missed her head. Still, she did not move.

She continued to sit there on that exposed bough, completely unperturbed in the morning light. It seemed as if she were surrendering herself to me. Then, as if nothing else mattered in the world, she began to sing. As I listened with the gun still to my shoulder, her voice seemed to grow louder and fill the branches of the tree with summer music. She blended perfectly with the bird-symphony coming from other trees. I looked once more at her brown iridescence, lowered my gun, and then turned and walked away. That was the last time I ever went hunting.

Listening for the Truth

We are all born intensely curious creatures. We are truth-seekers. In the beginning, the truth which interests us concerns the world and our place in it. So we spend our childhood and early adult years gathering facts and absorbing conventional wisdom. But there comes a time when we realize that knowing the "facts" isn't enough. They always bring us up short because they cannot show us the way out of pain. It is this realization that leads us to become more concerned with *experiencing* truth than with "knowing" facts.

The earnest search for what is true is always born out of crisis. D.T. Suzuki, the scholar/mystic responsible for introducing Zen to the Western world through his many marvelous books, once wrote,

> *The religious consciousness is awakened when we encounter a network of great contradictions running through our human life. When this consciousness comes to itself we feel as if our being were on the verge of a total collapse. We cannot regain the sense of security until we take hold of something overriding the contradictions.*[1]

But this "something" is so damn elusive. As soon as we try to grab it, it slips through our fingers. At the point we think we know the truth, we can be sure we don't know it at all. Truth moves swiftly and silently within a cloud of unknowing, showing itself only in brief moments when we least expect to see it. Just like my beautiful sparrow, truth hides best when it is hotly pursued. But if we stop for a moment and become perfectly still, truth will reveal itself in surprising ways. And we may be changed by the glimpse.

Most of us don't know how to stop and be still, and we don't really believe it could make any difference anyway. It doesn't make sense. All we really know how to do is listen to our brains chatter endlessly, even in our sleep. And the chatter of our thoughts hides the truth we have always known from our conscious minds. Instead of looking inward to the Source of truth, we search for it frantically in relationships, politics, business, and possessions. We may even search for it in church. Yet it always seems to remain just beyond our conscious understanding—which, of course, is exactly where it is.

Eventually we have to create our own version of the truth based on our particular thoughts and experiences. The world is just too scary not to. Unfortunately, our egoic version of the truth can never be completely true. Why? Because you can't create truth. You can only discover it. So we unconsciously distort our perceptions of the world in order to support our distorted beliefs. Then we spend our lives nurturing these illusions and defending them against all comers. To be proven wrong in our perception of truth means to be diminished, to run the risk of "death." This we cannot allow. So we judge, condemn, and attack those who are not like us, who do not share our vision of reality because they have their own vision to defend.

We could continue this game of cosmic hide-and-seek indefinitely if it weren't for one small problem. Our firmly held and vigorously defended illusions will always bring us pain. Always. In fact, the more fiercely we cling to our illusions of reality, the more it hurts. It's a bit like squeezing a porcupine with both arms for fear it will get away from you.

Now for the good news. It is in our moments of greatest anguish that truth is able to break through our barriers and reveal itself to us in some unexpected way. At first we may feel mocked by such glimpses. We may not be able to bear the light that illuminates the distortions upon which we have based our lives. So we learn to push away awe and wonder and to ignore our deepest emotions in order to remain safely nestled in the womb of our pain. In our fear and shame, we may even try to destroy that which is true and good. We may try to shoot the bird or crucify the Christ. But our attack on the Bringer of Truth, who is always our brother, can only be an attack on ourselves. In our anger and shame, we will succeed only in visiting more pain and suffering upon our own heads. But there is a chance that some of us might start listening to the birdsong in the trees and be humbled by our encounter with Reality. We may even lower our guns, bow our heads, and turn once more towards Home.

The Message of the Patriarch

Last Christmas my parents bought our two boys their first BB guns. Nancy and I were ambivalent about it but decided to let the guys try it out to see if they could handle the responsibility. On Christmas day, I took them out behind our house, set up some paper targets on the fence, and taught them how to shoot. I told them about all the rules of gun safety just as my father had told me. They listened just as seriously and intently as I had.

After they finished shooting their packet of BB's, I took them up to the patio under the giant sweet-ball gum tree that shades the west side of the house. As we stood there in the dappled sunlight, I asked them to listen quietly for a couple of minutes and tell me what they heard. I saw them look at each other with that half-amused expression they get when they know they're in for another story. Not wanting to disappoint them, I told about the sparrow with the yellow tint on her beak. When I finished talking, we all listened for a moment to the music coming from the branches above us.

MEDITATION: *Listening to Life*

Life, nature, the cosmos has much to say to us about the nature of Reality and our true identity within the All. We just need to remember how to listen. But so often, when we are confronted with the immense mystery of creation, we suppress our natural response of awe and wonder. It seems that life can make us feel so small and insignificant by comparison—at least until we stop imagining ourselves to be separate from it.

Try this meditation. Have someone read it to you, if possible, or read it yourself onto a tape and then play it back. Now, find a comfortable and quiet place to sit down and relax. Try to keep your posture erect, so that your spine is straight but not rigid. Focus for a few moments on your breathing, allowing the breath to move in and out naturally, until you feel more centered and relaxed. Close your eyes and try to imagine the following situation. Picture the details as best you can and actually place yourself in the scene. Feel free to change the details in any way to suit your needs.

You are walking barefoot along a beautiful stretch of beach. It may be a beach you have actually visited or one you simply imagine right now. It is fairly deserted, with only a few people walking in the distance. You are alone, but not lonely. It feels so good to just walk along the water's edge by yourself. Feel the warm sun as it shines down on your shoulders. Smell the salt in the air. And listen to the waves. Hear them as they crash and roll and make their way towards shore, just as they've done since the beginning of time. Now feel the cool ocean breeze coming in from the water, caressing your face and blowing through your hair. In this eternal moment, there is nowhere else you need to be, nothing else you need to do.

As you continue to walk along, imagine yourself playing "tag" with the water, just like when you were young. Sometimes you let the water come up over the tops of your feet so you can feel that cold, tingling sensation. Other times, you dance out of the way at the last second so the water can't reach you. And you smile softly to yourself, remembering.

Look out beyond the breakers, to where the afternoon sun is reflecting itself in the gentle ripples. It looks like thousands of diamonds, scattered carelessly across the waters by some wealthy and benevolent Deity. As you continue to watch the dancing light, let yourself remember the ancient truth that you are a part of everything you see—and, in some mysterious way, it is all a part of you.

Look down the beach about fifty yards and see the child of about five or six years who is playing alone in the sand. Now walk up to the child slowly, and when you are fairly close, stand and watch him or her play for awhile. Try to catch a glimpse of the expression on this child's face. Look into his or her eyes. What do you see there? Now watch as the child stands up slowly and begins to walk toward you. Notice the crumpled piece of paper balled-up in the child's right hand. When the child solemnly offers this piece of paper to you, as if it were a gift of inestimable value, accept it silently.

As the child disappears down the beach without a word, unfold the crumpled piece of paper carefully and read the message that has been written on it, just for you. Now, read it again. Listen to the waves crashing towards shore and feel the ocean breeze in your hair. And remember.

■

5

LAUGHING AT OURSELVES

The personal ego of man [sic] forms itself out of the impersonal life of the universe like a wave forming itself out of the ocean. It constricts, confines, restricts, and limits that infinite life to a small finite area. The wave does just the same to the water of the ocean. The ego shuts out so much of the power and intelligence contained in the universal being that it seems to belong to an entirely different and utterly inferior order of existence. The wave, too, since it forms itself only on the surface of the water gives no indication in its tiny stature of the tremendous depth and breadth and volume of water beneath it.

PAUL BRUNTON

As you proceed through life, following your own path, birds will shit on you. Don't bother to brush it off. Getting a comedic view of your situation gives you spiritual distance. Having a sense of humor saves you.

JOSEPH CAMPBELL

I WAS ALMOST seventeen years old before I saw the ocean for the first time. Perhaps I was old enough to really appreciate its magnitude and power; or maybe I was still young enough not to rely on rational, scientific explanations for what I was seeing and experiencing. Whatever the reasons, I have a need to return to the ocean from time to time to be reminded of my Source.

During most of my childhood years, we lived in eastern Washington State, about 250 miles inland; and a trip to the ocean was not a high financial priority for my lower-middle-class family. In addition, my parents didn't really like to travel that much. My father made his living as a collection and repossession agent for various department and appliance stores, and his work routinely took him all over the western states. Needless to say, he wasn't eager to jump back into the car for a weekend family outing after driving several hundred miles during the week.

Then in 1967, just after I entered high school, we moved west of the Cascade Mountains to within some eighty miles of the Pacific Ocean. We still did not go to see it. I don't think my mother was too crazy about sand. Sand isn't neat and mom likes neat.

In the summer of my seventeenth year (sounds like the opening to *Summer of '42*), my parents gave me permission to go on a weekend retreat with the youth group from the church my next-door neighbor attended. It took quite a bit of pleading and a little guilt manipulation ("You know, I'm already almost seventeen years old and I've still never seen the ocean!") but they finally relented. This was no small accomplishment as my father was known to be somewhat protective. For instance, when I was thirteen, he forbid me going fishing with my buddies because "You guys will start messing around, someone will throw you in the water, you'll hit your head on a rock and drown." Can't argue with logic like that.

Anyway, what I didn't tell my parents concerning this beach trip was that I had a crush on a certain twenty-year-old in that youth group, and she was the main reason I wanted to go. I'm sure this knowledge would have put my father over the edge. Sometimes parents just can't seem to understand the priorities of youth. At least that's what my kids tell me.

It was a bright and beautiful Friday morning when about twenty of us loaded our clothes and sleeping bags on the Trinity Lutheran Church (Missouri Synod) bus and headed for Cannon

Beach, Oregon. I don't remember much about the journey except that it was bumpy and very noisy. Everyone was laughing, talking, and carrying on like typical teenagers anticipating the fun and freedom of an entire weekend away from parental authority. Of course, they had all seen the ocean before and could hardly believe I had not. The other thing I remember about that two-hour drive to the beach is that about halfway there I "put the moves" on the twenty-year-old. I reached over and held her hand.

I can also vividly recall the exact place on the highway where I caught my first glimpse of the sea. That moment is as present to me now, complete with thoughts, feelings, and sensations, as it was some twenty-four years ago. As the church bus came over a rise and around a bend in the road, I saw it! The late-morning sun was glinting off the waves as they rushed toward the shore like blazing starbursts. I stuck my right hand out the bus window to feel the breeze, heavy with the pungent aroma of salt, blowing in from the water. I could not even begin to grasp the size of this ocean, as it seemed to reach into infinity. I felt as if my breath would be swept away on the sea breeze, so powerful and overwhelming was its majesty. If I had ever entertained any reasonable doubts about the reality of God, they were banished forever in that moment. As the bus rattled on, I fell silent for the next several miles, unable—or unwilling—to speak lest I break the spell. In that self-imposed silence, I ceased to exist as a mind full of questions, a body full of hormones, and a heart full of youthful self-doubt. There was only the sea.

That weekend at the beach flew by at an amazing speed. We went swimming, we played volleyball, we talked about girls, and we took long walks on the sand. But no matter where I was or what I was doing, I couldn't take my eyes off of the ocean. It kept drawing my gaze like a long-lost lover. Every night, after everyone was in bed, I would slip out and walk down to the edge of the water. I sat for hours in the chill, night air and listened to the rhythm of the waves as they broke gently and rolled up onto the sand.

On our last night there, the moon was full and slung low in the sky. It cast its reflected radiance in a golden path that extended from the shore to the horizon. It looked as if someone had laid a great band of shimmering yellow silk gently upon the waters. As I sat there in the mist, hugging my knees for warmth, I began to cry. Even now I find it difficult to express in words what I was feeling at that moment. It was as though I had lost myself and yet I was found. I was a part of the moonlight and the ocean and sky, and it was all a part of me. I had finally found my way home.

I left there unable to look at the world in quite the same way ever again.

The Anointing

Five years ago, I took my wife and two sons back to Cannon Beach to spend a week of our summer vacation and to torture my children with stories about my first visit to the ocean. We all had a great time. We swam every day and had bonfires on the beach every night. From the balcony of our condo, we could see the entire expanse of beach and look right out at Haystack Rock, a huge formation that sits about a hundred yards from the shore. During low tide, we all waded out to Haystack where the kids could explore various grottos and tidepools. During the afternoons, when the sun began streaking the horizon, I often sat on the balcony and stared out to sea.

One day out on Haystack, I climbed to a higher point on the seaward side of the rock while Nancy and the boys looked at the hundreds of brightly colored starfish in the tidepools. I walked to the edge of the point, about twenty or thirty feet above the water, and watched the waves crashing on the rocks below. Though surrounded by beauty, I felt despondent. About a month prior to our vacation, I had finished correcting all the galley proofs and writing the index and glossary for my first book. Not more than two weeks later, I received word that the publisher who had agreed to produce it had gone out of business. This meant I would again have to go through the long and humbling process of placing it with a publisher, as I did not have an agent. In addition, I was informed that my manuscript and original graphs would not be returned to me until I paid all the expenses of production to that point. I was disappointed and feeling sorry for myself.

As I stood there on that wonderful rock, inhaling the salt air and feeling the mist in my face, I could feel myself longing for another Glimpse like the one I had on this beach when I was seventeen. I just wanted to feel close to God again. I wanted a renewed sense of vision and purpose so I would know my life was making a difference. And I wanted to stop feeling so depressed. I remember looking out towards the horizon and praying to God (like that's where God lives) that I needed some assurance I was on the right track and He was still guiding my steps. I asked Him to forgive my weakness and impatience and to remind me once again of those things that are really important in life. What I really wanted to say was "Why the hell did you let this happen to my book!" It would have been much more honest if I had.

I remember lowering my eyes from the horizon and asking God to give me some kind of a sign—something that would confirm He loved me and had a special place for me in His plan (like maybe a dove descending from the heavens or something). Of course I was thinking about the powerful impact I might one day have on the world if I could just find a way to get my writing into print. It was all very dramatic, and I was taking myself quite seriously. As I turned to go back and join Nancy and the boys, I didn't feel any better inside. If anything, I felt worse. At that precise moment, a low-flying seagull happened by and deposited his entire previous evening's meal on the top of my head. Apparently seagulls do not have the same rules about bathroom behavior that we do. Talk about adding insult to injury: I had just been communing with God in my favorite natural setting, only to wind up wearing seagull crap.

I started to wipe the gooey mess out of my hair and curse the day I had ever discovered this stupid beach. But before I had a chance to really get into feeling indignant, something broke loose inside of me. I don't know what it was or how it happened but I started laughing. I don't mean smiling or grinning or chuckling. I mean belly laughing. I laughed so hard people began to gather their children away from me as I walked by. I wanted to tell them not to worry because I was a psychologist, but I don't think anyone would have believed me. Or maybe they would have. When I told my wife and kids what had happened, they started laughing too. The four of us laughed together all the way back to the condo.

The Best Medicine

That bird with the fully-functioning gastrointestinal system reminded me of a very important truth. Laughing at ourselves feels *really* good. It is an unbelievably effective ego solvent. Each time we let go and surrender our egoism enough to be amused at our own folly, we dissolve away a little bit more of the illusions and pretense that separate us from the knowledge of our true identity. Too much seriousness can blind us to the absolute mystery and wonder of our own existence. Laughter is a mechanism through which we can lead ourselves to a deeper understanding of our origin and nature. It allows us to abandon the illusions of our separateness from life and alienation from God so we can be immersed once more in our Source. As Jean Houston once wrote,

> At the height of laughter the universe is flung into a kaleido-scope of new possibilities. High comedy, and the laughter that ensues, is an evolutionary event. Together they evoke a biological response that drives the organism to higher levels of organization and integration. Laughter is the loaded latency given us by nature as part of our native equipment to break up the stalemates of our lives and urge us on to deeper and more complex forms of knowing.[1]

I take myself far too seriously. I am often guilty of thinking what I say or do in this life is somehow of supreme importance.

And I can become quite impatient with those who do not appreciate this fact. Such personal pomposity only serves to erect a veil between the little self I think I am and the Unity of Being that is my real Self. Laughter lowers the veil a fraction of an inch so I can catch a Glimpse of a higher Reality, a more noble truth

6

KNOWING THE TRUTH

When the Self is no longer identified with the ego, when, in certain spiritual practices, it penetrates and realizes its own depths, it simply knows that it is eternal and all-inclusive. Words can convey no proof, no conviction, of this experience. But, when realized, this knowledge is of a certainty so much greater than any other kind of knowledge that doubt seems impossible.

ALAN WATTS

What he [sic] takes to be his true identity is only a dream that separates him from it. He has become a curious creature which eagerly accepts the confining darkness of the ego's life and turns its back on the blazing light of the soul's life.

PAUL BRUNTON

IN THE PAST, I have complained that mystics and contemplatives are never specific enough about the stages of the spiritual journey: They tend to rely heavily on myth and metaphor to describe their encounters with what they insist is an ineffable Reality. I have even implied that they've been holding out on us. Well, I may have been a little hasty.

I have since discovered there really is something about "ultimate truth," whatever that may be, that does not lend itself well to discursive language and logical thought. Perhaps this is because the intuitive part of our mind which is able to apprehend such things is not good with words. Fine. I would just like to know whose idea it was to hide Truth in the deaf and dumb section of our brains. Do you ever wonder if the gods are having fun with us on this one? Wouldn't it have been so much easier if they had just published the answers to life's transcendent mysteries in *Reader's Digest* so we could read about them in the bathroom? Be that as it may, and with all due respect to past generations of mystics, madmen, and Zen masters, let me tell you another story.

A Parable of Light

There once was a young man who lived in a far country where only a very few people in any given generation ever witnessed an actual sunrise. As strange as this may seem, it was not because the people were naturally lazy or because they just didn't care about sunrise. On the contrary, most of the citizens of this great land were extremely industrious and responsible and tried very hard to provide a good life for themselves and their families. In addition, most of them believed in the existence of Sunrise and many of them went to church on Sundays to learn more about the indescribable beauty and eternal holiness of Sunrise. But it had become their custom, handed down over countless generations, to retire late in the evening and sleep until noon of the following day.

No one could actually remember how this custom got started and most people didn't really care. Someone at the state office was quoted as saying one time it had something to do with harvesting crops by moonlight in order to avoid the heat of the day. Of course no one had farmed in these parts for over fifty years. In spite of this, everyone still lived their lives according to this ancient rhythm. Shop owners usually opened for business about 2:00 P.M. and closed at 10:00 P.M. Midnight was the normal dinner hour and school children did not have to go to bed until 3:00 A.M! Of course they still whined to stay up later.

This particular young man was a typical product of his cultural conditioning. He had grown up witnessing many marvelous sunsets because he was always awake at that time of day. But like the rest of his contemporaries, he had never seen the Sunrise because he could not seem to change his normal sleep patterns.

Over the years he had heard a couple of age-wizened people talk about Sunrise. They always got this strange, far-away look in their eyes as they tried to describe the pristine beauty and incomparable inspiration of actually witnessing Sunrise. But words always seemed to fail these venerable "Witnesses," and they would usually end their conversation by lowering their heads and muttering unintelligibly, as if in prayer.

The young man had read many books about Sunrise. He could also remember hearing his parents tell stories about them in hushed and reverent tones throughout his childhood. Although everyone he knew seemed to accept the existence of Sunrise without question, the young man had a rather empirical and skeptical bent of mind and couldn't quite let himself believe in Sunrise for the simple reason that he had never seen one. And try as he might, he just couldn't seem to awaken himself early enough to see if they were real.

A few of his young friends agreed with his "intellectual atheism" concerning the existence of Sunrise; but most people thought he was foolish or crazy or even evil for not believing in them. He soon learned not to talk about the subject of Sunrise often except to simply say, "As for me, I've never seen one." But in the depths of his heart and mind, the young man secretly hoped they were real.

This young man spent the next few years getting on with the business of life. He married his high school sweetheart, had two beautiful sons, and worked hard at his chosen vocation as an electrical engineer. He also became very active in various charitable and community service organizations which seemed to take up most of his free time. He coached his sons' Little League teams and was the leader of their scout troop. He was also the first man to serve three consecutive terms as President of the Society of Electrical Engineers (S.E.E.). By every external criterion, he was a great success.

But the young man, now somewhat older and wiser, still had a feeling of emptiness and incompleteness that haunted him whenever he had a quiet moment to reflect. It occurred to him this ache he felt in his heart from time to time was his long-buried and almost forgotten longing to see the Sunrise. He talked it over with his wife, who expressed a similar longing, and they decided to start attending a church where the preacher spoke about Sunrise almost every week. So one Sunday afternoon, they packed up the kids (which was no small task in itself) and headed off for the 3:00 P.M. services at Our Lady of the Holy Sunrise Church. They arrived just in time to hear the sermon.

After several months of attending this church, the young man started to feel somewhat better. He began to believe Sunrise might exist, though he had yet to see it for himself. It was very easy to believe because everyone else in the church believed it too. Of course, none of them had the discipline necessary to rise early enough to catch a glimpse of the Sunrise. Lacking any direct experience of their own, everyone in the church, including the young man, became dependent on the minister's personal beliefs and perceptions concerning Sunrise. Most of the time this was fine with the young man. But there were occasions when he wasn't quite sure if the minister had actually seen the Sunrise for himself or if he was simply reporting what he had heard from his professors in seminary.

These thoughts and questions didn't bother him too much, because the preacher was a good and sincere man whose eloquence had inspired the young man's heart and mind to the point that he now firmly believed in the reality of Sunrise. He and his family became very involved in various church activities for the next several years. His children were all baptized and then confirmed as "Sunrise Servants" which made the young man feel very happy and proud. He often told his kids inspiring stories about Sunrise just as his parents had told him. For the most part, the young man was content with his life—as long as he stayed busy.

Then something upset the carefully constructed balance of his life. Perhaps he or someone he loved became seriously ill, or maybe there was a death in the family. I never heard the details. Whatever it was, it caused the ache in his heart to return with more intensity than he could ever remember. It was an experience that was almost impossible to classify. At times it felt like a physical pain that clutched tenaciously at his heart; at other times it was like the intense longing for an absent lover.

He found himself praying and meditating more often and he read every book on Sunrise he could find. One day he came across a passage in a book that made him weep like he had never wept before. The words went something like this:

When you find the Light within you
You will know that you have always
Been in the center of wisdom.
As you probe deeper into who you really are
With your lightedness and your confusion
With your angers, longings and distortions
You will find the true living God.
Then you will say
I have known you all my life
and I have called you by many different names.
I have called you mother and father and child
I have called you lover.
I have called you son and flowers.
I have called you my heart.
But I never, until this moment,
called you Myself.[1]

Over a period of several months, the young man became increasingly distracted and self-absorbed—to the point that the fraternal brothers of S.E.E. asked him to resign as president. He also stopped coaching baseball, much to his sons' dismay, and spent almost every weekend reading alone in his study at home. His wife, who was also beginning to feel quite neglected and unappreciated, asked him to go with her for some marital counseling. He grudgingly agreed.

One day, the young man heard the educational channel was going to broadcast from a well-known museum in a far country. They were planning to show a number of famous paintings and other works of art depicting Sunrise. So great was his excitement, he called all of his friends and family together to watch it in his home. He even taped it on his VCR so he could replay it from time to time. The TV station did a marvelous job, and everyone was greatly impressed. The young man, who was now middle-aged, watched the program over and over in awe and wonder. While the ache in his heart was greatly reduced, the longing to actually see Sunrise with his own eyes remained stronger than ever.

His family and friends worried that he was becoming far too obsessed with this desire to see the Sunrise. For them it was enough to simply believe. They did not understand his intense need to see the Truth for himself. For this man, belief was no longer enough. He had to know.

Several more years passed and the no longer young man was beginning to show the signs of age. For example, he now had to drink decaf coffee and it took him more than thirty minutes in the shower every afternoon to get the kinks out of his back. His children were all grown and had wives and families and successful careers of their own. His oldest son was a psychologist and his younger boy had become a very well-known actor. The man and his wife were still in relatively good health and were beginning to actively plan for their retirement. His wife was very excited about visiting the Grand Canyon on their first post-retirement vacation, as the man had always been too busy with other things to take his family there.

One morning he awoke somewhat earlier than usual. As he went downstairs to put on the coffee, he looked out his living room window and caught a fleeting Glimpse of the Sun just as it cleared the horizon. He could not believe his good fortune at having come so close to seeing the Sunrise, and his heart was filled with joy. Over the next couple of years he had several more Glimpses, and each time he felt tremendous peace and unity. He redoubled his efforts to awaken in time to see the entire Sunrise; but it seemed the harder he tried, the more miserably he failed. Finally, in despair, he gave up trying.

One winter morning, when the man was quite old, he awoke suddenly as if from a bad dream. He looked at the radio alarm on his wife's nightstand and saw it was a full hour before Sunrise. He jumped out of bed without regard for the arthritis in his knees, threw on his clothes, and raced downstairs. In his excitement, he began running from room to room trying to decide which window would give him the best view. Finally he decided to go outside because he didn't want his view to be distorted even by a pane of glass.

As he stood bare-footed in the frosty grass of his front yard, he watched as the Sun began to peek over the eastern horizon and fill the morning sky with light and color. He was totally transfixed by the sight and quite unaware of the cold wind blowing through his thin clothing. It seemed as if his entire body was itself suffused with light and that he had somehow become completely submerged in the dawnlight all around him.

For the first time in his life he felt completely at peace, as if he had finally returned home after a long and difficult journey. The vague sense of fear and disquiet that had nagged at his mind all of his life was completely gone. He could not decide whether to weep for joy or to laugh uproariously, and so he simply watched in profound silence. The only thought that occurred within the calm serenity of his mind was, "It is so simple, so amazingly simple!"

When the Sun had risen some distance from the horizon and the frost on the grass had completely melted, he turned towards the house with the sure knowledge that he could never be the same again. For he was no longer just a believer. He had finally become a Knower.

From that day until the day he died, the man spoke very little of his experience. For those few he met who had seen Sunrise for themselves, words were unnecessary. For those who came seeking his wisdom, words were totally inadequate. Sometimes he would tell them stories and parables about awakening from their nightmares and dispelling all of their illusions and fears. At other times, he would just lower his head and mumble a prayer in response to some seeker's intense questions. But usually he would look at them with compassion in his penetrating blue eyes and exclaim, "Go, see for yourself! It's really so simple!"

The man died at a very ripe old age with a prayer on his lips and a twinkle in his eye. His wife, children, and grandchildren lovingly laid him to rest in the family plot at the local cemetery. In accordance with his instructions, the simple headstone bears no name and no dates of birth and death. It is inscribed only with a picture of the Sun peeking over the mountains on a frosty winter morning.

The Quest for Transformation

It would seem amidst the noise and chaos of our mental and emotional lives, we all yearn for a place of internal quietude and peace. I think we are all tired of being afraid. We are tired of being a solitary self that must stand alone in a universe of pain and separation. We want to stop hurting and quit feeling guilty. We want to awaken to our true place in the cosmos and to our true identity within the All. In metaphorical terms, we want to see God, the Sunrise, for ourselves, to *know* I AM more intimately than the boundaries of a simple religious faith can ever allow. Like Jacob wrestling with the angel, Arjuna talking with Krishna in his chariot, or Buddha meditating under the Bodhi tree, we want our lives and our consciousness to be transformed completely and forever. Nothing less will suffice to end our perfidious sense of alienation.

The path to psychological and spiritual transformation is well-hidden and cannot be negotiated by the endless twisting and turnings of the logical and analytical mind. To glimpse this forgotten land, we must abandon our educated and sophisticated egos and return to our essential simplicity. We must learn once more to immerse ourselves in myth and allegory, intuition and silence. We must demand to see the "face of God" for ourselves, as Moses did on Mount Sinai. We need a direct revelation, a private viewing. Only then will we be able to rouse ourselves from sleep quickly enough to catch the first rays of the Sun as it rises within our soul.

7

BEING AND DOING

Zen tells man that he is free now, that no chain exists which he needs to throw off; he has only the illusion of chains. Man will enjoy his freedom as soon as he ceases to believe that he needs to free himself, as soon as he throws from his shoulders the terrible duty of salvation.

HUBERT BENOIT

To do anything involves the ego. And if you recognize you need do nothing, you have withdrawn the ego's value from your mind. Here is the quick and open door through which you slip past centuries of effort, and escape from time. To do nothing is to rest, and make a place within you where the activity of the ego ceases to demand attention. Into this place the Holy Spirit comes, and there abides.

A COURSE IN MIRACLES

FOR those of you who haven't guessed it yet, I'll say it straight out. I have a compulsive personality. Really, it's true (Nancy is groaning in the background). I have grown up with the belief that life should proceed in an orderly and predictable fashion and that things should be neat and organized. A place for everything and everything in its place . . . and all that jazz. I really think I have my mother to blame for this curse. She used to have me remake my bed because the lines on the plaid bed-spread weren't straight. See, Freud was right. It is our parents' fault.

In addition to my moderate compulsiveness, I have also nourished the insane belief that when I want something done "correctly," I should just do it myself. As a result, I am now a card-carrying, compulsive workaholic who doesn't delegate tasks easily. Fortunately, this isn't so bad in the real world (except for the heart disease, of course). Society tends to reward this particular brand of neurosis with some measure of recognition and success.

But it doesn't seem to work with God at all. I know. I've been trying it for years. Compulsiveness, competitiveness, control. These have never been big words in the spiritual lexicon. No, God seems to like words like surrender, self-forgetfulness, unconditional forgiveness, receptivity, and loving abandon. These are exceptionally tough words. My ego doesn't like them or what they stand for, and it tries hard to convince me they're not really necessary for true spiritual attainment. Yet I have recently begun to believe maybe they are.

Muscular Religiosity

I began my spiritual journey at the age of thirteen when I became "born again" in a relatively conservative Protestant church. Since that time, I've learned that most conservative Christian organizations have a few simple rules for their members to follow. Here are the three most common ones.

1. Be Born Again. Accept Jesus Christ as your personal Lord and Savior and make a public profession of your faith (that means to tell people about it). Then follow the Lord's example by being baptized by the method of total immersion (absolutely no sprinkling allowed) in the conservative Christian church of your choice (or the river Jordan).

2. Imitate Jesus Christ. If it feels good, don't do it. I repeat: Don't do it! Don't dance, don't drink, and don't smoke (unless you are a deacon and were raised in North Carolina). Furthermore, don't go to R-rated movies or date girls who chew tobacco (no matter where you were raised). And if someone from Texas asks you if you believe in biblical inerrancy, smile and say, "Amen brother!" That should get you off the hook until you have time to look up the word "inerrancy."

3. Minister to Others. Participate in every activity the church offers and be there whenever the doors are open (the bare minimum is twice on Sunday and once during the week). The Lord will richly bless your life as you dedicate your time and energy (and ten percent of your income) to Him. Remember, every day sinners are dying and going to hell (and to Oklahoma). Quality family time is optional.

Now, I think Rule #1 for a conservative Christian is really fine for the most part—as long as you remember that the language is meant to be understood metaphorically, and that it is completely acceptable for people in other religious traditions to symbolize their spiritual experiences with different metaphors. Of course, that rather verbose last sentence is enough to get me placed on any number of conservative Christian prayer lists across the country.

Having come to appreciate the spiritually symbolic value of Rule #1, the other two rules remain quite unpleasant. They are very similar to the unwritten but strictly enforced rules of many other conservative, non-Christian religions, with only minor historical and cultural variations. In other words, this is not a problem of a particular faith or denomination. This is a universal problem of the human ego whenever it decides to go to church.

Let me explain what I mean. During my undergraduate years at California Baptist College, I took Rule #3 very seriously (I repeatedly broke Rule #2 because Nancy chewed tobacco). I was involved in an unbelievable number of activities, all aimed at ministering to others in the name of the Lord. They were also aimed at improving my status in the Christian community and earning me special favor in the eyes of God. Of course, I never admitted this even to myself. As measured by these two rules, I was quite possibly one of the best Christians on campus (B.C.O.C.).

By my senior year, my "Compulsive Christian Project" had escalated to an unbelievable point. In addition to working thirty hours per week as a night stock clerk at a grocery store and carrying a full-time course schedule during the day, I was also:

- President of Campus Student Ministries, the largest student activities organization on campus. (Minimum time commitment: fifteen hours per week.)
- Student representative to the Curriculum Committee of the college faculty.
- Chairman of the Student Committee on Chapel Programming.
- Director of the Student Center at one of the local Baptist churches every Friday and Saturday night. (Minimum time commitment: twelve hours per week.)
- High school boys' Sunday School teacher.
- Children's Church Director.
- Volunteer chaplain, Riverside County Hospital.

Enough of my resumé. You get the picture. I had no idea at the time what I was trying to prove, but it very nearly cost me my faith. At the end of my senior year, I had what I would call a mini-mid-life crisis (a precursor to the "Real McCoy" I would have a few years later). In spite of all my academic and religious "accomplishments" (Rule #3) and all the effort I had put into controlling and redeeming my more selfish thoughts and desires (Rule #2), I could still feel that cold emptiness inside whenever I spent more than two minutes alone with myself. This was my first real experience with the futility of projects, especially religious projects.

I don't think I blamed my situation on God, at least not consciously. And I certainly didn't blame it on myself (I could have saved myself a lot of time here). So the only thing left to blame for my unhappiness was the church. After all, I had done absolutely everything it recommended for establishing and maintaining a meaningful and growing relationship with God. In fact, I had done it in spades. After all of that effort, I didn't even feel as close to God as when I was thirteen. I was really at a loss as to what to *do*. More than once I can remember fasting all day and praying all night for God to make Himself real in my heart and mind. Nothing happened. Nothing. Unfortunately at that time in my life, I didn't know how to interpret NOTHING.

Even though I had been raised in a religious tradition based on God's free and unconditional grace, I was still trying to earn my own way. And I AM couldn't make Himself heard over the buzz-saw noise of my ego which was in the frantic process of doing "His work." I wanted Him to speak louder and He wanted me to be still. I didn't get it. After graduation, Nancy and I didn't darken the door of a church for more than five years.

Now in spite of this and many other frustrating experiences with my Christian project through the years, I still believe there is a certain amount of effort and discipline required of us early in the spiritual quest. For a period of time, we must do battle with our ego, which is fully capable of being both extremely noble and unbelievably selfish. We must struggle to subdue its natural desires for power and recognition and discipline its selfish actions by conscious effort.

In mystical language, this is called the "Long Path" approach to truth. It's a little like doing hard time in the Old Testament where the Hebrews wandered in the wilderness for forty years. We have a little wandering to do ourselves. Think of it as spiritual conditioning. It is essential we learn the disciplines involved in thinning and purifying the ego and detaching ourselves from our fears and illusions if we are to ever return to the complete awareness of our Source. Sometimes we will succeed in getting the ego to behave itself. Perhaps we will learn to be more loving or more patient in certain situations. But as with the children of Israel, there will be more times when we will fail. No one can be on guard all the time. Besides, the ego can be an incredibly subtle and elusive adversary.

But here's the paradox. As necessary and useful as this battle with our ego may be, there will come a day when we must leave the fray. We will have to stop fighting against our weaknesses and give up striving to improve ourselves. After serving our "forty years" in the long path wilderness, we have to make an *effortless* transition to the "Short Path" and wait patiently for the movement of grace. Otherwise the ego will live on—new and improved to be sure—but alive nonetheless. Where there is effort, there is ego. And where there is ego, there is pain. As Paul Brunton writes,

> *The Long Path creates a condition favorable to enlightenment, but since it is concerned with ego, it cannot directly yield enlightenment. For its work of purifying the ego, however necessary and noble, still keeps the aspirant's face turned egoward. . . . Everything that he accomplishes in the way of self-improvement, self-purification, or self-mastery is accomplished by the force of the ego. No higher power, no grace of the Spirit, no faith that transcends materialism is needed for these things. Whatever it is, and however beneficial it be, reform of the ego's character will not lead directly to the destruction of the ego's rule. For although the ego is willing to improve or purify itself, it is not willing to kill itself.*[1]

The problem with salvation or enlightenment by "muscular" self-effort is not that it makes us bad people or that we will one day burn in hell for our foolishness. It simply doesn't work. It cannot take us to our final goal of unification with the Logos. Even though our character may improve, we remain enmeshed with the dynamics and projections of the ego. Because *doing* anything, even reforming the ego, requires the force and strength of the ego itself. And there's the rub. Any effort I expend in trying to weaken or surrender my own ego will only serve to build it up even stronger than before. In other words, self-effort can never rid us of our self so that we can rediscover our true Self.

The Apostle Paul once pointed out that the ego (he called it the flesh or the old man) lives according to the "law of sin and death." He could just as easily have called it the law of strenuous self-improvement. Obedience to this law of the ego may improve our image and train us in some necessary disciplines, but ultimately it will turn our quest for Reality into simply another project. And as we have discussed before, ego projects can never lead us into the promised land. They can take us right to the border, but no further. Just like Moses, the ego is forbidden to enter paradise.

All of this begs the question, "What then must we do to be saved?" How do we learn to stop listening to the clamor of the ego and start identifying with our higher Self? If there is a God in heaven, then happiness and peace of mind must be real and attainable in this life. If not, then the gods are truly crazy, and existence is as absurd as the Existentialists tried to tell us. If it is true that we can know Perfect Peace here and now, then the beginning of our quest must be the painfully honest admission that we have lost our way in the far country. Our ego project has failed miserably to provide our lives with meaning and purpose of an enduring kind. And this is true even when our efforts have been aimed at conforming ourselves to the example of the Logos. It only takes one moment of honest, self-conscious despair to set our feet on the path towards Home. In such a "holy instant," we will hear the voice of God whispering quietly in our ear, "You are loved and you are forgiven. Everything you could ever hope for is already accomplished. Stop trying so hard." As Paul Tillich once wrote,

> *In the midst of our futile attempts to make ourselves worthy, in our despair about the inescapable failure of these attempts, we are suddenly grasped by the certainty that we are forgiven, and the fire of love begins to burn. That is the greatest experience*

anyone can have. It may not happen often, but when it does happen, it decides and transforms everything.[2]

Effortless Spirituality

The key to salvation, enlightenment, or awakening is this: there is *absolutely nothing* we must do. We must throw off the terrible duty of our own salvation and accept what has already been done and what has always been true. This is what the Logos in all of its incarnations throughout history has always come to teach us. Lighten up, listen, and you will know who you are. It has always been our frantic *doing* that has rendered us deaf to that "still, small voice" that speaks to us eternally about our place in the Mind of God.

Because we are so used to the constant battle in our minds between conflicting thoughts, feelings, and sensations, we may need considerable practice to learn how to be mentally quiet. Meditation and contemplation are the only disciplines I know that can teach us this skill of one-pointed concentration. As said in *A Course in Miracles,*

The memory of God comes to the quiet mind. It cannot come where there is conflict, for a mind at war against itself remembers not eternal gentleness. The means of war are not the means of peace, and what the warlike would remember is not love. . . . Brother, the war against yourself is almost over. The journey's end is at the place of peace. Would you not now accept the peace offered you here?[3]

The most important virtue on this journey towards Buddha-Mind, Christ-mindedness, or God-consciousness is not hard work and discipline, although they certainly have their place early in the quest. Rather, it is the simple faith necessary to believe that a God you have never seen, utilizing methods you could never understand, will surely lead you to that knowledge of ultimate things you could never put into words.

The second most important virtue is the patience and humility

to let God deliver us in His own way and in His own time. As St.
Peter once said,

> *Humble yourselves, therefore, under the mighty hand of God,
> that He may exalt you at the proper time, casting all your anxi-
> ety upon Him, because He cares for you.*[4]

In this context, humility implies the willingness to place ourselves under the guidance or tutelage of God, to adopt a
"beginner's mind" that is free of preconceived notions and self-
satisfied efforts. From this place of complete safety, we can "cast
our anxieties upon Him," and develop the quietude of mind
that is so necessary for the reduction of fear and the attainment
of salvation or enlightenment. To quote again from *A Course in
Miracles*,

> *How instantly the memory of God arises in the mind that has
> no fear to keep the memory away! . . . The trumpets of eternity
> resound throughout the stillness, yet disturb it not.*[5]

Or to paraphrase Peter's words,

> *Place yourselves humbly under the tutelage of God without any
> ideas about what you know or don't know. In this place of
> perfect safety, let the peace of God gently enfold you and quiet
> all of your anxieties. And at exactly the right moment, He will
> awaken you.*

Of course, all of this takes time—perhaps an entire lifetime.
If you are Hindu, it could take several thousand lifetimes. Now
you know why I'm Presbyterian.

So we learn to chill out. We start reading enlightening books
and scriptures, and we learn to train our minds in attentive silence through daily meditation practice.

But what happens when we become impatient with I AM's
sense of timing? What happens when the ego decides to take
matters into its own hands again and help God along? We will
probably dive once more into our projects and get busy with

doing. Only this time we will have to repress and deny any awareness of our own arrogance and foolishness and work even harder to convince ourselves of the holiness of our intent. Such increased self-deception is necessary because we already know too much. We mount our trusty white horse, lift our banner high, and go on another mission *for* God. This is the kind of energy that gave us the Crusades and the Spanish Inquisition. Just remember as you and your ego ride off into the sunset— any mission undertaken *for* God is really a mission *away from* God.

Going Along for the Ride

One of the advantages of living in Southern California is being never more than a few miles from Disneyland. When the boys were younger, we took them quite often. One attraction we always had to visit was Mr. Toad's Wild Ride. This is a storybook ride in Fantasyland which involves moving through a series of sharp turns, slamming doors, and mock explosions in a small replica of a Model A Ford. It's not much of a ride for adults but kids seem to love it.

I'll never forget one trip when Adam was five or six years old. We waited the obligatory sixty minutes in line and then boarded the ride. Nancy took Chad with her and I kept Adam. I placed him on the driver's side of the car so he could pretend to drive.

For the first half of the ride I didn't pay much attention to what was going on. I noticed Adam turning the wheel back and forth furiously through the various sharp turns, and I smiled to myself knowing he was having such a good time. That is until I saw the look on his face. His eyes were wide with terror and he was white as a sheet. There were tears rolling down his cheeks as he clung tenaciously to the steering wheel. After an instant of confusion, I knew what was wrong. Adam thought he was really driving the car! I grabbed him up quickly and put him in my lap. I could feel his little body shake as he began to weep. I whispered over and over, "It's alright sweetie, you weren't really driving. There's no danger, Adam. See, the car is following that track. It's okay. You don't have to be afraid." By the time the ride was over, he understood and began to relax.

I think this is how it is for us. We believe we're actually driving the car and are therefore responsible for how everything turns out. And this scares us to death. We need to understand that our lives are not under our conscious control. They are following a track laid down before time began by a Wisdom that lies deep within us. We don't have to work so hard. All will be well. Stop striving, breathe deeply, and pay attention. But most of all, enjoy the ride. That's why you came here in the first place.

MEDITATION: *Flowing with the Tao*

There is much in our culture and in our own individual experience that leads us to believe we must constantly set future goals, work diligently towards those goals until they are achieved, and then strive earnestly to reach the next set of goals. This is the Western formula for success in life. It's also the Western formula for chronic pain and anxiety. It's a bit like climbing a knotted rope in gym class. You strain heroically to pull yourself up the rope so your feet can reach the next knot and give you a moment of blessed relief. After a short rest, you start out again, accompanied by the cheers and jeers of your supporters and detractors down below. You pull yourself painfully toward the next knot, even though you know very few people ever reach the top. This is the philosophy of the ego, which can only exist in its own imagination as long as it is cramped and in pain.

The goal of the spiritual life is detachment and surrender. We are to let go of the ego's insane insistence on pain and discomfort (which it can cleverly disguise as "the search for happiness"), and become more mindful of the many ways in which it creates these conditions through grasping and aversion.

Close your eyes and try to imagine the following scene (after you have read through it once). You are swimming in a beautiful mountain river. The water is as blue as the sky, and the temperature is perfect on this warm summer day. The shoreline is dotted with Ponderosa pines and there are snow-covered mountains in the distance. Every once in a while, you see a deer or a bear wander down to the river's edge for a drink of cool, clear water.

Although you have been swimming for some time, you begin to notice that the scenery on the shore has not changed much. There's that same ancient pine off to your left, its trunk scarred and blackened by a forest fire. It has been right there for the past several hours. But how can that be? You've been swimming steadily the whole time. You also begin to notice how cramped and tired your muscles feel. But you put the pain out of your mind and continue on, swimming even faster, with a strong, purposeful stroke.

Several hours later, when your mind is numb and your body is completely exhausted, you are suddenly struck with the realization that you are swimming upstream! You have made absolutely no progress because all of your efforts have been equally matched by the force of the river's current. After a few moments of anxiety and confusion, you decide to turn your body around and float downstream on your back.

Your muscles relax, your mind clears, and you begin to admire the passing scenery. You notice that the sky isn't just blue, it's subtle shades of blue and grey, azure and white. Every tree along the shore speaks to you of its own unique character and history, and every animal seems a creature of great delight. Your own mind becomes a tremendously interesting process, as you watch your thoughts arise and pass away as easily as the clouds gliding overhead. And you marvel at the growing sense of peace and equanimity in your heart as you keep floating down the river.

Sometimes the current runs slow and deep, like the sap of a tree on an autumn morning. Feel the power of it as it bears you along. At other times, the current runs swift and noisy through shoals and rapids. This is when we are all tempted to turn around and start swimming upstream again. But don't. It hurts too much. Just trust the current. Sink down into its womb-like stillness, and let it carry you to the sea.

■

8

MEDITATION

The gift of learning to meditate is the greatest gift you can give yourself in this life. For it is only through meditation that you can undertake the journey to discover your true nature, and so find the stability and confidence you will need to live, and die, well. Meditation is the road to enlightenment.

SOGYAL RINPOCHE

Enlightenment is not something you achieve. It is the absence of something. All your life you have been going forward after something, pursuing some goal. Enlightenment is dropping all that. But to talk about it is of little use. The practice has to be done by each individual. There is no substitute. We can read about it until we are a thousand years old and it won't do a thing for us. We all have to practice, and we have to practice with all of our might for the rest of our lives.

CHARLOTTE JOKO BECK

I DON'T know many people who meditate. In fact, I don't know many people who even know what meditation actually involves. I used to think meditation meant you had to sit funny, make weird noises, and believe in a lot of New Age nonsense. I figured people who meditated regularly either lived in monasteries or spent all their free time at Esalen (and you know what *those* people are like). Yet every major religious tradition throughout history has placed meditation at the top of the list of important spiritual disciplines, often before prayer or the study of scriptures. Unfortunately, meditation has become a lost art for most people in the modern western world regardless of whether they are religious or secular in their orientation.

Being in Your Right Mind

I'm not sure why we in the West essentially abandoned meditation practice. It may have something to do with a confluence of factors such as the Renaissance, the Reformation, and the Industrial Revolution. Most historians and social scientists agree that the combination of these unique historical patterns has contributed to an overemphasis on the logical/analytical and language-generating capabilities of the human mind. These abilities are believed to be controlled by the left hemisphere of the brain and have been progressively disciplined and developed to the neglect and even exclusion of the mind's more emotive and intuitive functions. As a result, we have become a culture of left-brained, Newtonian scientists and rugged individualists who only trust logic and our own strenuous efforts. And we systematically train our children to do likewise. Psychiatrist Anthony Stevens speaks of this left-brain domination of our culture in his book, *Archetypes: A Natural History of the Self.*

> *Ever since the Renaissance, stress has increasingly been laid on the need to develop left hemispheric functions at the expense of the right. Encouragement of the left hemisphere begins early in life with the emphasis placed in all Western primary schools on the need for proficiency in the Three Rs (writing, reading and arithmetic). Although right hemispheric activities such as art, drama, dancing and music are given a place in curriculum, fewer resources and fewer hours are allocated to them than to left-sided disciplines such as mathematics, languages, physics and chemistry; and at times of economic retrenchment it is invariably the right-sided activities which are pruned or curtailed.*[1]

The right hemisphere of our brains controls that realm of human consciousness that is primarily responsible for synthesis, holistic perception, and the intuitive integration of meaning. These functions make possible such things as imagination, creativity, symbolic and metaphorical understanding, spiritual inspiration, and most forms of artistic expression and appreciation. But as Stevens correctly points out, these right-brained abilities are no longer accorded much value in our consumer-oriented culture. The institutions of an industrialized society, including its educational and religious institutions, tend to emphasize only those mental activities that can solve practical problems or produce tangible, economic rewards.

This one-sided and fragmentary development of our minds over the past few hundred years has made it possible for us to create a technologically advanced society that can put a car in every garage, a computer in every office, and a man on every moon. In terms of economic growth and technological innovation, we in the West have far outdistanced our brothers and sisters in the rest of the world. But there is a price to pay for such left-brained prowess. Not only do we continue to plunder Mother Earth of her resources and replace them with ecological filth in the name of progress, but we begin to forget about our intimate connectedness to Father God. Just as the Earth is the source of our sustenance, God is the source of our Being. The left hemisphere pays little attention to either of these truths. As Abraham Heschel wrote,

> *Normal consciousness is a state of stupor, in which sensibility to the wholly real and responsiveness to the stimuli of the spirit are reduced. The mystics, knowing that man is involved in a hidden history of the cosmos, endeavor to awake from the drowsiness and apathy and to regain the state of wakefulness for their enchanted souls.*[2]

It is reasonable to assert that a group of people, a nation, or an entire world will eventually lose touch with any intimate knowledge and experience of the Holy in direct proportion to how much they undervalue and neglect to develop their intuitive and expressive abilities. As our consciousness becomes more and more specialized, our lives will become more fragmented, rigidified, and neurotic. All that will be left to us in terms of spiritual understanding will be a fundamentalist intolerance of deviation from a set of narrowly defined standards and a blind adherence to concretized religious doctrine and extremist political creeds. This literalization of truth is the only kind of "religion" the left-brain is capable of creating: one in which language and logic are the most important, if not the only, modes of apprehension and understanding. In such an atmosphere of illusion and intolerance, ego projects run wild; and people inevitably end up killing their environment and each other in order to defend their individual perceptions of the truth. Our very survival on this planet may well depend on whether or not we learn to balance human consciousness with an equal emphasis on right-brain functioning.

Mystics and contemplatives of every religious persuasion tell us the same thing about the path to God. They have always emphasized that human beings can never understand or approach through discursive intellectual concepts an ineffable God who is the Ground of Being. In other words, I AM completely transcends the dualistic machinations of the left side of our brains. This means we can not experience higher consciousness or enlightenment and move from the darkness of uncertain belief to the garden of secure knowledge simply through the use of our words and ideas. The very thing in which we usually place our highest confidence, our discursive intellect, can never take us beyond the beginning stages of the spiritual journey. No matter how hard we may try, we just can't get there from here.

The right hemisphere, with its holistic and intuitive abilities, provides a corrective balance and empowers the fullest expression of human consciousness in our individual experience and in the world. Only through developing our right-brain functioning, and subsequently integrating both hemispheres (symbolically represented in the world's mythology and psychology as the marriage of masculine and feminine energy), can we begin to experience our Oneness with each other and with all of creation. This experience is essential if we are to learn a new tolerance for one another and a new respect and concern for our fragile biosphere. It is also necessary if we are ever to take the final step towards meeting God in the tabernacle of our own expanded consciousness.

Right Practice

Unfortunately, most of us in the West have forgotten the "technology" for developing and experiencing the aspect of our consciousness that would eventually enable us to discover a more complete sense of our cosmic or transcendent Identity. Meditation and mindfulness practice *is* that technology, and enlightenment is the practical realization of that identity. But a practice that involves sitting still for long periods and learning to quiet the mind in order to encounter Truth does not exactly fit our current cultural Zeitgeist—and isn't likely to attract many devotees. As Karen Armstrong points out,

> *The God of the mystics is not easy to apprehend. It requires long training with an expert and a considerable investment of time. The mystic has to work hard to acquire this sense of the reality known as God (which many have refused to name). Mystics often insist that human beings must deliberately create this sense of God for themselves, with the same degree of care and attention that others devote to artistic creation. It is not something that is likely to appeal to people in a society which has become used to speedy gratification, fast food, and instant communication. The God of the mystics does not arrive ready made and prepackaged. He cannot be experienced as quickly as the instant ecstasy created by a revivalist preacher, who quickly has a whole congregation clapping its hands and speaking in tongues.*[3]

Meditation will never be the way of the masses. It isn't stimulating enough to attract a crowd. It is for those people in every generation who have grown weary of their normal way of being. It appeals to those who have tried the solutions offered by secular materialism or relationships or organized religion, and have found them bereft of any lasting ability to deliver on their promises of inner peace and temporal happiness. For those with the insight to finally understand the futility of projects, meditation practice offers a new and deeper way to seek the Truth within. It requires time and discipline and some special training to be sure, but so does everything else we have tried on this journey. As we have seen, ego projects require a tremendous amount of time and energy and lead only to despair. The big difference is that meditation is *right* practice; it is a kind of "non-striving effort" that is effective in bringing us back to ourselves.

Getting Started

When you first begin to meditate, it will seem you are getting nowhere, simply because meditative silence is so foreign to our normal mode of consciousness. Your mind will wander endlessly to a thousand different "left-brained" thoughts in the space of a moment, like a wild monkey on speed. You will become frustrated and may even feel depressed and defeated from time to time. Be patient with yourself. Treat your mind like a mischievous child, with firm love and gentle persuasion. Each time it wanders, bring it back easily and without recrimination to the particular focus you are using that day in your practice. As you continue to practice regularly and patiently, you will find your mind gradually becomes more disciplined and obedient and more able to concentrate on one perception or awareness at a time.

You will also notice with continued practice that your mental burdens will slowly begin to drop away. Situations you used to constantly worry about and try to control will seem far less important or compelling. Fear and anxiety will begin to diminish, leaving behind a deep and abiding feeling of tranquillity and well-being. You will feel more connected to the other people you encounter in your life, relating to them more as brothers and sisters than as strangers in a strange land. And you will start to recognize and experience the divine essence that is vibrantly present in every aspect of life, engendering within your heart a renewed sense of childlike wonder and respect for the created order. Your life will become more like the uninterrupted flow of a mountain stream, neither good nor bad but simply clear and imperturbable and in harmony with the highest Reality. Sogyal Rinpoche, the well-known teacher of Tibetan Buddhism, speaks eloquently of these non-dualistic experiences that are often experienced in meditation when he writes,

> *To meditate is to make a complete break with how we "normally" operate, for it is a state free of all cares and concerns, in which there is no competition, no desire to possess or grasp at anything, no intense and anxious struggle, and no hunger to achieve: an ambitionless state where there is neither acceptance nor rejection, neither hope nor fear, a state in which we slowly begin to release all those emotions and concepts that have imprisoned us into the space of natural simplicity.*[4]

These qualities are inevitable results of practice, superb "fruits of the spirit." They have been verified in the living experience of hundreds of thousands of people throughout history and can become a part of your life as well. If the idea of this type of practice beckons to you, if it seems to draw your soul towards itself with a gentle insistence, then meditation may be the next important step on your journey towards Home. If so, grab your zabuton and your zafu (meditation cushions) and let's get started.

Place and Posture

In the beginning of practice, it is probably best to meditate in a comfortable and quiet room relatively free of external distractions. The mind is unruly enough without adding outside interference such as traffic noise and children's voices. As your practice continues, you will find external stimulation gradually loses its power to distract your concentration, and you will be able to meditate under the most difficult of circumstances. I also recommend that you choose a room that can be special, and that you meditate in that same room (or corner of a room) every day if possible. In this way you will invest a positive energy in the room and begin to create a "sacred space" that will bring you peace and soothing relief from the normal concerns of daily life each time you practice there. This will also enable you to enter into meditation more quickly and effectively. Joseph Campbell speaks of sacred space this way.

> *A sacred space is hermetically sealed off from the temporal world. When you're in such a space, there is no penetration through the enclosure. You are in an eternal zone that is protected from the impact of the stimuli of the day and the hour. That's what you do in meditation: seal yourself off. The meditation posture is a sealing-off posture, and the regularized breathing furthers your inward-turned explorations. The world is sealed off, and you become a self-contained entity.*[5]

Different schools of meditation recommend different positions for the body. These range from the full-lotus position of advanced Yoga practice (ouch!) to the Japanese tradition of sitting on a low wooden bench with a padded seat. Every tradition emphasizes the importance of sitting with the spine straight, like "a pile of golden coins," in order to reduce the number of distracting thoughts that continually enter the mind.

I find sitting cross-legged on the floor (the Burmese position) with a small cushion under my tailbone is a very comfortable and well-grounded posture for my practice. Cushions filled with cotton batting are best for meditation because foam rubber tends to be too "squishy." Try to elevate your tailbone enough so your knees are flat on the floor. This gives you a solid and secure connection to the earth beneath you. Don't worry too much if you experience pain in your legs (it should pass within a few years!) but be careful not to stretch the muscles too quickly. The pain will move in and out of your awareness and you will gradually become more limber as you continue to practice. In the meantime, you may want to do a few stretching exercises each day before you meditate. Remember to keep your back as "straight as an arrow" but not rigid, and tuck your chin under just a little in order to straighten and stretch the vertebrae in your neck.

There are also several different hand positions that have been utilized over the centuries. I prefer the traditional Buddhist method of placing both hands in your lap, palms upward, with the left hand on top of the right. Let your hands curl naturally and then gently place your thumbs together to complete the circle of energy. Let your hands rest easily next to your abdomen, about two inches below your navel. This is the area known in Yoga practice as the *hara*. It is one of the most important energy centers or chakras in the human body. As you breathe normally, focus your attention on your hara by imagining you are breathing in and out of that region into your hands. This will help to ground you with a lower center of gravity and ensure you are breathing deeply from your diaphragm.

As you begin your meditation session, pick out a spot on the floor at about a forty-five degree angle along your line of sight or approximately two feet in front of you. Stare at that spot for a few moments and then gradually allow your eyes to unfocus and close about half-way. Do not close your eyes completely. It is helpful to keep your eyes at least partially open so you don't become drowsy and so your imagination does not begin to create all sorts of visual distractions on the inner screen of your mind.

As contrived and uncomfortable as these suggestions may seem to you at first, remember they have been proven effective over centuries of meditation practice in various religious traditions throughout the world. Use this same posture every time you meditate. Feel free to stand up, stretch, and walk around slowly every few minutes, if needed. Before long, this posture will begin to feel completely natural; you will be able to meditate for extended periods of time with very little attention to your physical being.

Concentration Techniques

There are literally hundreds of different philosophies and techniques of meditation currently being taught around the world. They range from the calm awareness of Vipassana meditation to the mentally demanding koan practice of Zen to the physical demands of Hatha Yoga. In spite of their many differences, these various approaches share two important characteristics.

First of all, most schools of meditation endeavor to develop an increased sense of internal peace and/or insight that will ultimately lead to the gradual or sudden attainment of *satori* or enlightenment. In other words, they all share the same basic goal. Only in this enlightened state do all our fears of life and death and our perpetual striving for immortality cease. Our ego project vanishes into thin air as our ego is transformed and absorbed into the eternal Self: We are finally able to see clearly through the painful illusions on which we have based our existence and can experience directly the truth of our Oneness with all Being. Satori is the necessary beginning of real life. It is the salvation or "second birth" that the Logos always embodies and recommends. Religious doctrines and rituals are judged effective only by how well they symbolize this spiritual journey and by how insistently they point the devotee in the direction of this new birth of consciousness. As D.T. Suzuki writes concerning the sudden attainment of enlightenment that is the sole aim of Zen practice,

> *In Zen there must be a satori; there must be a general mental upheaval which destroys the old accumulations of intellectuality and lays down a foundation for a new faith; there must be the awakening of a new sense which will review the old things from an angle of perception entirely and most refreshingly new.*[6]

Suzuki echoes the prosaic words of Jesus Christ when he spoke to Nicodemus about spiritual transformation.

> *Jesus answered and said to him, "Truly, truly, I say to you, unless one is born again from above, he cannot see the kingdom of God." Nicodemus said to Him, "How can a man be born when he is old? He cannot enter a second time into his mother's womb and be born, can he?" Jesus answered "Truly, truly, I say to you, unless one is born of water and the Spirit, he cannot*

enter into the kingdom of God. That which is born of the flesh is flesh, and that which is born of the Spirit is spirit. Do not marvel that I said to you, 'You must be born again.' The wind blows where it wishes and you hear the sound of it, but do not know where it comes from and where it is going; so is everyone who is born of the Spirit."[7]

Meditation can be seen as a technology for the attainment of higher consciousness or an enlightened state of awareness, an inner map that will lead the serious seeker to the top of the Mount of Transfiguration and clothe him or her in the glowing raiment of the Logos. This technology usually involves some form of systematic and progressive instruction for training the mind in the difficult art of silence and concentration. This is the second characteristic that most schools of meditation share: They each in their own way involve the aspirant in the practice of concentrated awareness and mental discipline. This is usually accomplished by focusing intensely and mindfully on such things as a koan or word puzzle, a particular thought or verbal expression, or a bodily sensation.

Here again, the options are almost infinite. I recommend the following methods of mental focusing simply because I have found them to be most effective in my own practice.

Focusing on the breath. This is one of the oldest methods of meditation and is found in almost every school of practice. It involves allowing your attention and awareness to rest easily and mindfully on the rhythm of your breathing. It is a good technique for beginners because it excludes all reasoning and puts the discriminating mind to rest. And since our breath is always with us, we can meditate anytime and anyplace.

Begin your practice by locating the place in your body where you are most aware of the physical sensation of the breath. Some people feel it in the nostrils, some in the chest, and others feel it most obviously in the abdomen. Once you have located them, focus on these sensations and begin mentally counting both halves of your breath in the following manner. When you inhale, count "one." When you exhale, count "two." The next inhalation would be "three," and so on. Count up to ten and then start over. Focus on your breathing and on the numbers as you say them softly in your mind. This technique gives your mind something simple to focus on and enables it to become progressively more quiet. But remember, training the mind to be quiet and aware takes much time and practice. This is what meditation is all about. Try not to become frustrated by the endless stream of distractions your mind will attempt to generate for you. None of these distracting thoughts will be an impediment to your practice unless you discriminate between them, seeing some as "good thoughts" and others as "bad thoughts," and then invest emotional energy in trying to keep some and get rid of others.

The ego exists only as long as you are identified with the discriminating thoughts flowing endlessly through your consciousness. These judgmental thoughts are born of the belief in separation instead of the simple and immediate awareness of unity. Your ego thinks it will "die" if it allows you to enter into the silent Void. And in a sense, it will. But the ego doesn't understand that "death" is always followed by transformation or resurrection, so it lives in constant fear of silence and peace. It tries to keep you in a condition of contraction and pain where fear and anxiety rule your mind. It is only when the ego is in pain that it truly knows it exists.

If the ego can't keep you away from meditation completely by presenting you with an endless array of "important" tasks that must be accomplished each day, it will fill your mind during meditation with a meaningless phantasmagoria of thoughts and ideas. If this should fail to hold your attention and dissuade you from practicing, the ego will simply distract you by becoming angry or frustrated with its own inability to concentrate properly! Learn to recognize these subtleties of the ego. Practice patiently every day, no matter how many other tasks you have to accomplish. And each time you notice your mind wandering and making distinctions, do not cling to the "good" thoughts or try to expel the "bad" ones. Simply bring your mind back without recrimination to an awareness of the numbers and the rhythm of your breathing.

As your practice proceeds over several days, you may advance to the method of counting only the inhalation of each breath. The first time you inhale, count "one." Then exhale. The next inhalation would be "two," and so on. Count up to ten and then start over, just as before. After several more days of this second method, you will be ready for the more difficult task of counting only your exhalations. Breathe in. Then as you exhale, count "one." Breathe in again, and as you exhale, count "two." Count to ten, as always, and then return to one.

Finally, after several weeks of practice, you will be ready to focus on your breathing without counting the breaths. Simply let your mind follow the subtle nuances of each inhalation and exhalation. As Joseph Goldstein and Jack Kornfield suggest in their excellent book on insight meditation, *Seeking the Heart of Wisdom,*

> *Keep your attention clearly focused on the sensations and feelings of each breath. Be with the breath at the place in the body where you feel it most clearly and distinctly; the rising and falling of the abdomen, the movement of the chest, or the in and out at the nostrils. See how carefully and continuously you can feel the sensations of the entire inhalation and exhalation, or the entire rising-and falling-movement. . . . Let the awareness be soft and relaxed, letting the breath come and go in its own rhythm. . . . Be with it as it reveals itself, aware of how it goes through various changes.*[8]

When random thoughts intrude, as inevitably they will, bring your attention calmly back to your breathing. If you find your mind is wandering more than usual in a given session, simply return to one of the preceding methods of counting your inhalations or exhalations for a few rounds of ten. This should calm your mind enough to continue with the practice of observing your breath without the use of numbers.

Focusing on an object. Some people are more visually ori-
ented and find it useful to focus their attention during formal
meditation on an object they find both beautiful and meaningful. This might be a flower or the flame of a candle, a sparkling
crystal or a photograph of a sunset over the ocean. The important thing here is that you choose an object you find inspira-
tional and which brings you a feeling of calm serenity when
you contemplate it. Many teachers recommend the use of a
painting or a small statue of Christ or the Buddha or some other
recognized master. This is a way of both focusing the mind and
inspiring the heart with the flame of love and devotion.

Place the object you have chosen to contemplate on the floor
in front of you so your line of sight is about forty-five degrees.
As you begin to meditate, look intently at the object or picture
and allow your mind to enter into that state of calm awareness
that is free of all judgments and attachments. Allow random
thoughts to arise and pass away of their own volition without
your concern or intervention. Imagine yourself becoming one
with the object of your contemplation so there is no longer any
difference between "this and that" in your mind. Then simply
abide in the eternal presence of God.

Focusing on a mantra. A mantra is a syllable, a word, or a
phrase that is chosen for its special meaning to the aspirant,
usually as a result of his or her religious orientation. It is repeated silently in the mind or quietly verbalized in order to
bring the mind to that place of peace and serenity that is meditation. The definition of mantra is "that which protects the
mind." And so it does. A mantra protects us from the agitation,
anxiety, and negativity that is so typical of normal mental functioning by providing us with a focused thought of tremendous
spiritual power. It purifies our attention, reconditions and re-
fashions our consciousness, and leads us inexorably forward in
our journey Home to the Father. Mahatma Gandhi once wrote,

> *The mantram becomes one's staff of life and carries one
> through every ordeal. It is not repeated for the sake of repetition,
> but for the sake of purification, as an aid to effort. It is no*

empty repetition. For each repetition has a new meaning, carrying you nearer and nearer to God.[9]

Mentally repeating the mantra with great concentration during formal meditation and at other times throughout the day is a technique that has been widely used for thousands of years in most traditions including Buddhism, Christianity, Hasidism, Sufism, and Hinduism. Each of these religious traditions has its own customary mantram. In Christianity, for example, the most widely used mantra is called the Holy Name. For those who yearn to become more like Christ, the name of *Jesus* is repeated slowly and reverently. Other Christians may use *I Am that I AM* or just *I AM*, the name God declared to Moses. In the Greek Orthodox Church, the Jesus prayer, *Lord Jesus Christ, Son of God, have mercy on me*, is the most widely used mantra. Sometimes this prayer of Jesus is shortened to just *Lord Jesus Christ*.

Jewish mystics throughout the ages have used two very powerful mantram. *Barukh attah Adonai* means "Blessed art thou, O Lord," and *Ribono shel Olam* translates "Lord of the universe." The Sufi mystics of Islam have often used *Allahu akbar*, "God is great," or simply *Allah, Allah*. And for Buddhists, *Om mani padme hum*, which signifies "the jewel in the lotus of the heart," is the most commonly repeated mantra.

A mantra should be chosen with great care and consideration; and once it is selected, it should not be changed or set aside under any circumstances. There will be many times, especially in the beginning of your practice, when you will be tempted to abandon your mantra because it doesn't seem to be working. This is actually a trick of your ego, and it signifies that you *are* getting somewhere. Otherwise, the Trickster in your own mind would not be so worried. So when you choose a mantra, choose wisely. It is going to be with you for quite some time. Think about the meaning and implication of the words contained in various mantram and your own subjective response to them. Do they have significance for your life? Do they seem to turn your mind inward? Is this mantra a part of your own religious heritage and is that good or bad for you?

Once you have decided on a mantra, let it be your mate for life. It will lead you to the very depths of your own identity.

Finally, do not try to create your own mantra. While there is nothing particularly wrong with this, you will be unnecessarily depriving yourself of great spiritual power. Choose a mantra that has been sanctified and empowered by long use, one that has the proven ability to awaken men and women from the nightmare of their normal consciousness. The roots of such mantram go down deep into the collective unconscious where they gather tremendous transformative power over the countless generations of their use in ways that we will never quite understand.

The mantra that I chose early in my practice is *I AM*. During formal meditation, I repeat this holy name slowly in my mind with as much concentration as possible. I imagine shooting my mantra like an arrow into the deepest layers of my mind so as to release its healing and transformative power. When I am feeling particularly distracted, I say the words out loud a few times at the beginning in order to move more quickly into my meditation. Sometimes I coordinate the mantra with my breathing, mentally saying *I* as I inhale and then *AM* as I exhale. At other times in meditation, I do not try to coordinate the mantra with my breathing but just allow both to proceed naturally at their own pace. Throughout the day, whenever I feel tense or exhausted, I will take a few moments to silently repeat *I AM* in my mind. Before long, I will once again feel the peace and renewal of meditation. I also repeat my mantra at times when I am engaged in a mechanical activity such as walking, cleaning the pool or garage, or brushing my teeth. By utilizing our mantra in this way throughout the day, we can begin to break down the dualistic barrier between the peace and fluidity of meditation and the contraction of our daily lives.

Dealing with Distractions

Let's say you've been practicing meditation diligently for several months and your ability to concentrate has increased markedly. You're sitting there one day on your custom-made cushion and everything is going well. Your body is completely still and your mind is almost totally quiet for the first time in days. You're following the sensations of your breath without words and without effort. You are in a state of meditative bliss that is deeper and more encompassing than you have ever experienced. All of a sudden, the thought arises, "I wonder what we're having for dinner tonight." Poof! The "spell" is broken and you begin thinking about all the different foods you like to eat. After a few moments of culinary revelry, you notice that your mind is wandering and so focus once more on the sensation of the breath in your nostrils. The bliss returns. Then you think, "Wow, it sure didn't take long for the relaxation to return when I caught my mind wandering! I didn't even have to count. I must be getting better at this meditation thing. I wonder how much longer until I'm completely enlightened." Woops. Back again to the breath, following the sensations effortlessly as they flow along like pure water of a mountain stream. "I wonder . . . is my meditation time is about up?" And so it goes.

This is how the mind operates, shifting constantly from one thought to another in a conditioned chain of neuronal impulses consisting of past memories, current experiences, and future fantasies. It is this chaotic stream of interwoven thoughts that we mistakenly identify as ourselves. But these thoughts should not be seen as a problem to be conquered during formal meditation practice. We mustn't think of them as the enemy. They are, in fact, the whole point of the exercise. Learning how to deal skillfully with these distracting thoughts enables us to explore and gain insight into the ways in which our mind reinforces the illusion of ego. Such mindfulness allows us to gradually break free of our identification with this endless stream of discursive chatter so that we can awaken to a much deeper understanding of ourselves.

In Buddhist methodology, distracting thoughts are divided into five different categories. Because of its directness and simplicity, the typology is useful regardless of your religious orientation or the type of meditation you practice. We will consider each of these categories separately even though the methods for dealing with each type of thought are much the same.

Craving and Desire.   Suppose you are sitting in meditation one morning and nothing is going right. Your knees hurt, your back is getting stiff, and your mind is completely out of control. Then you remember one day last week when your meditation was particularly serene and you find yourself wishing it were that way every time. Wouldn't it be great if meditation—or all of life for that matter—was always blissful? Why can't we just live life on the upside, on the inbreath, all the time? Why does there have to be pain and discomfort?

This is desire. It leads to the universal ego-pastime known as grasping (in America we call it consumerism). We think we can end our discomfort or pain by obtaining some circumstance, relationship, or emotional state that we currently do not possess. The ego doesn't understand that grasping is itself a source of pain because it is, by definition, insatiable. It is like trying to grab a handful of smoke. Nothing we desire and seek to obtain can fill the emptiness we create by imagining that we, who share fully in the bounty of the Eternal, could possibly lack for anything.

When you become aware of thoughts of desire, try to notice how and when they arise in the mind. Are there physical sensations that accompany these thoughts? Notice the mental/emotional state that is created by grasping. How familiar is that state and how intense is it this time? Notice how long it lasts and watch it as it finally passes away. Then return your attention easily to the sensations of your breath.

Aversion.   Desire and aversion are endpoints of the same continuum. While desire leads to grasping after thoughts, feelings, or experiences we find pleasant or think we need, aversion leads to pushing away or avoiding whatever we define as unpleasant or painful. It could be an unkind word or action you feel guilty about in the past or a potential situation you fear in the future. It might be insecurity or depression you find yourself trying to reject and ignore. Here again, the ego doesn't get it that aversion itself is a source of great pain. Whenever we attempt to repress or deny our experience, refusing to accept gracefully whatever life may bring, we distort reality and set ourselves up for a more painful confrontation with that reality at a later time. It is inevitable.

Whatever the nature of the aversive thought, handle it in meditation the same as you did with desire. Notice the thought as it arises and note any sensations that are connected to it. Also notice the energy that is automatically generated to reject that thought or sensation. How intense is that energy? How long does it last? What does it feel like in your body? Then watch it pass away and return your attention to your breath.

Lethargy. As distractions go, this is my personal favorite. No matter what time of day it is or how energized I may feel, I can sometimes sit in meditation for five minutes and begin to feel like I haven't slept in a week. This is a great trick of the ego. If you insist on practicing a technique which systematically increases your ability to be mentally and physically still (which begins to dissolve the ego illusion), then the ego will just convince you to go to sleep. Not a bad strategy for a cornered ego.

Lethargy should not be confused with actual physical fatigue. If your body is really tired, get off your cushion and go to bed. Lethargy is a state of mind, not a physical state, that essentially shuts down our awareness and limits our mental acuity. It is the complete opposite of mindfulness (lucid awareness and attention) and it ranges in intensity from mild drowsiness to complete torpor. This mental state is closely akin to aversion. It is the ego's way of avoiding thoughts, feelings, or sensations that are boring, unpleasant, or painful. As a noted meditation teacher once said, "Lethargy is enforced stupidity pretending to be sleep."

The handling of lethargy is the same as for the other distractions. Notice when it arises (be sure to catch this one early!), how long it is present, and when it passes away. Then return to the breath. When your practice of mindfulness is not enough to deal with this hindrance, get up for a few moments and walk around or go outside for some fresh air. Then return mindfully to your cushion.

Agitation.   If this is not the most common category of hindrance for the beginning meditator, it is certainly the one most quickly noticed. "I just can't make my mind be quiet . . . it jumps all over the place!" "I can't keep my mind on the breath for more than one inhalation before I'm thinking about what I have to do tomorrow." "I can't believe how out-of-control my brain is all the time." These are all common laments of the beginner. It is important that you don't become discouraged by your first conscious encounters with the "wild monkey mind." Even experienced meditators have periods when their minds jump rapidly from one thought to another, refusing to settle on one thing at a time. Be patient. This is precisely the problem that meditation practice is designed to address.

Mental agitation produces a state of mind that is uncomfortable and unsettled, like the feeling of dread you get just before seeing the dentist. Try to identify this feeling state when it first arises. How strong is it? What is its characteristic texture? Notice how certain thoughts can increase or decrease the intensity or change the emotional flavor of this uncomfortable feeling. Imagine yourself moving into this state of agitation rather than trying to ignore or avoid it and then watch as it passes away. Return your attention to your breath.

Doubt.   "What am I doing here? Sitting cross-legged on a cushion, thinking about my breath is a complete waste of time. I should get up and do something tangible and productive. Besides, my knees are killing me!" These thoughts are categorized as doubt and they are very common. They have led many honest seekers to abandon their meditation practice, at least for a time. It is easy to understand why doubt can be such a problem. Meditation is a practice that is completely foreign to our normal state of consciousness, and it requires much time and dedication. This gives the ego plenty of ammunition to distract us from an activity it finds incomprehensible and vaguely threatening.

Doubts can be very difficult to resolve, so don't even try during your meditation period. Any energy you invest in actively trying to reason through these doubts or dispute them only gives them the energy they need to remain strong. Don't get involved. Deal with doubtful thoughts mindfully by taking a mental step backwards and watching closely. Observe the thoughts as they arise, watch how strong or persistent they become, and notice when they pass away. Then return your mind to the rhythm of your breath.

Further Considerations

I recommend people begin their practice with ten or fifteen minutes of formal meditation twice each day. Try starting with some moderate exercise, such as brisk walking, followed by meditation and a light breakfast (be sure to repeat your mantra mentally while you walk). You will find this regime sets a wonderfully peaceful and relaxed tone within your heart and mind that will make your day more enjoyable and productive. Then, just before you retire for the evening, meditate once again. You will sleep far more peacefully and awaken very refreshed for such a small investment of time. Over a period of several months, increase both of your practice times gradually until you can meditate for twenty to forty minutes twice each day. While this may sound like a lot of time to "sit and do nothing," you will be richly repaid with increased physical health and emotional well-being. And each day you will move closer to your own awakening.

You may use any of the techniques outlined above, or others you might have read about; but I recommend you start by counting the breath. This is a simple and straightforward method that is very effective for training the mind in one-pointed concentration. While you are practicing this technique, begin the process of searching out a mantra. When you have chosen one or are assigned one by a teacher, incorporate it gradually into your meditation. Then experiment with the contemplation of an object, preferably a statue or painting of the particular incarnation of the Logos that is recognized by your religious tradition. Once you are adept in the use of each of these methods, feel free to alternate your practice among them as often as you wish.

When your formal meditation time is over, do not rise too quickly to resume other activities. Linger for a while. Allow your mind time to make the transition slowly so it can transport the meditative state of deep serenity into your normal consciousness.

I have begun to suggest that people keep a meditation journal so they can record their observations of the experience and any insights they may have received from their higher Self. Keeping a journal not only enables us to track the course of our practice, it is also a natural way to make the transition back to normal activity. Be careful though that you do not spend time in meditation trying to decide what you will write down about it later! If this starts to happen regularly, throw the journal away.

I have one final suggestion. Read the mystics. Read them regularly and read them widely. Every religious tradition has its mystics and they all have seen the same Truth. Listen to them. Let their lives and experiences inspire you and lead you in the direction of Home. Emulate their examples and they will teach you about Reality. I also strongly suggest you read several books on meditation. This will expose you to a wide variety of techniques and approaches so you can creatively design your own practice. In addition to the study of scriptures, make the reading of books on world mysticism, meditation, and the spiritual journey a part of your daily life. This will serve to complement and deepen your practice significantly. It will also give you a number of sources for answering your own questions about meditation.

Meditation is a spiritual discipline that allows us to take the journey inward to a place of stillness and peace deep within our own minds. As the Apostle Paul said, "Let this mind be in you which was also in Christ Jesus." In metaphysical terms, meditation serves to permanently transform consciousness as the ego becomes sensitized to the call and direction of our true nature and is gradually reunited with our higher Self or the "Holy Spirit within us." To use the scientific metaphor, meditative practice enables us to access and integrate the higher intuitive and holistic functions of the right hemisphere as a corrective to the dominance of the discursive intellect. This integration accesses a numinous state of consciousness which enables us to open our hearts and reach out to others in authentic love. As Jack Kornfield writes in his wise and wonderful book, *A Path With Heart,*

> *This is meditation: To resume our true nature and discover an enormous sense of rest and peace, a spaciousness in our heart in the midst of life; to allow ourselves to become transparent to the light that is always shining. "It is not far away," says one Zen master, "It is nearer than near." This is not a matter of changing anything but of not grasping anything, and of opening our eyes and our hearts.*[10]

Claire Myers Owens describes the numinous state of enlightenment or awakening that is induced by meditation in these beautiful words.

> *The bliss and awe of enlightenment are indescribable. The whole experience of self-realization is ineffable because it is beyond the limits of reason and words—whether the method is one of induction, as in Zen, or spontaneous.*
>
> *The enlightened man [sic] emerges from this overwhelming experience a new person. A transformation of his character, behavior, and hierarchy of values has occurred. A new life style arises without his volition, astounding no one so much as the person to whom it happens. His ego has mysteriously diminished. He experiences a selflessness of which he did not know*

himself capable, a certitude for which he longed, a love of the human race that astounds him, harmony with the universe that his rational mind had assured him was impossible, and a joy unlike any other (as I discovered in my own spontaneous self-realization).

The enlightened person feels as if realization of the self answers all questions, dispels all doubts, abolishing fear and anger, hate and jealousy. It ends alienation. It brings a new kind of harmonious identity with the self, others, nature, and the universe. The rational mind becomes clarified, functioning with intuition—which is in harmony with the universal law.[11]

Further, she says,

For the enlightened man no longer desires wealth and fame and power. He is no longer compulsively attached to personal love and sensuous pleasures, prolongation of youth and beauty, or knowledge gained by rational methods. He no longer fears old age, sickness or death or poverty. His joy lies in his newly awakened Buddha-nature, his identity with universal Consciousness, his harmony with his fellow men, and his desire to serve them selflessly. He is at home in the universe.[12]

The techniques presented in this chapter have been gleaned from several different spiritual traditions, especially the Buddhist practice of Vipassana or insight meditation. Because they are not doctrinaire, these various forms of meditation can be adopted by anyone, regardless of religious orientation or denominational preference. These particular techniques emphasize the development of access concentration or one-pointed awareness which is necessary before you can progress to higher levels of insight. When practiced regularly, the requisite level of concentration can usually be achieved in a relatively short period of time, perhaps two or three months. Then you will be ready to add mindfulness practice, an ancient form of awareness and spiritual insight, which will be described in the following chapter.

9

MINDFULNESS

We leave reality for at least two reasons. One of them is that sometimes it is just so-so; other times it is painful. In both cases we leave: we go into a fantasy world in our heads, which provides a certain amount of immediate relief. The problem is that it then becomes automatic to leave all the time, to go off to fantasy places. Then, when we try to be in reality, we are fighting against years of accumulated habit.

CHARLES TART

Change begins when I do nothing except observe. The wisdom of the railroad crossing: Stop. Look. Listen. Meditation is the healthy form of voyeurism: My Self watches my ego. . . . The self-awareness that grows out of the habit of witnessing is nonjudgmental. I look at my actions, my feelings, my experience with soft and compassionate eyes, from a great distance as if I were God or a novelist. The chief rule of the witness is: Judge not. Do not identify with or against anything you observe.

SAM KEEN

LET'S BE honest with ourselves. We must be doing something wrong here because the normal state of human consciousness is just not that much fun. In fact, as both Christ and Buddha tried to point out, living in our normal state of mind is really quite painful. I don't know about you, but most of the time I try to blame my unhappiness and dis/ease on outward circumstances. When that doesn't work, I switch to blaming other people. But the external world isn't really the source of my problem, *I* am. While there is certainly no shortage of objective pain out there, *I* am the author and finisher of my own *suffering*. The sooner I figure this out, the better.

Since leaving the Garden, we have spent the majority of our time lost in fantasies and abstract ideas about what has happened in the past or what we anticipate may happen in the future. In effect, we are "lost" to the direct experience of what Paul Tillich called the "Eternal Now." Only rarely, as when we are surprised and temporarily overcome by the intensity of an awe-inspiring or painful experience, do we taste of the present moment. And the present is the only Real moment. It seems we would rather focus our time and attention on the unchangeable (and nonexistent) past, thereby inviting the pain of nostalgia or regret, or the unpredictable (and equally nonexistent) future, thereby immersing ourselves in chronic anxiety.

But wait, there's more. Living in an endless miasma of past and future fantasies is not our only source of suffering. Somewhere in the course of human development, we also became lost to the essential unity of all Being. We no longer directly experience our true nature, which is one with the One. Our everyday minds or "consensus consciousness," which is built on the very limited information of our five senses, bombards us with persistent testimony of our separateness and isolation from God, from one another, and from ourselves. We then invest tremendous reserves of mental and emotional energy refining this myopic sensual feedback into a stable identity in order to convince ourselves that we exist.

We want to be special and unique individuals who can stand alone in the universe. But there is a problem when we walk out of the Garden under our own steam: We end up standing alone in the universe. So much for the empty promises of the separated ego. Is it any wonder we all try to medicate away our deep sense of anguish and distress with innumerable activities, addictions, and attachments? I can imagine the eminent philosopher and social commentator, Bugs Bunny, looking at us all with the same disdain he normally reserves for Elmer Fudd and saying, "What a bunch of moroons!"

There is really nothing new in any of this. Every great spiritual tradition has identified these very same problems. Christians, Buddhists, Muslims, Jews—they may use different words and metaphors to describe the human dilemma because of historical and cultural differences, but the underlying meaning is the same. We have "fallen" from our original state of spiritual wholeness and perceptual innocence and have lost touch with our deepest Self in the here and now. So we live in a world of perceived separation and alienation. And these painful illusions are mostly of our own making. Each of these traditions also recommends solutions that are remarkably similar to each other when analyzed in the light of the Perennial Philosophy. What they all say is we must learn to become more *mindful* in order to remember who we are and where we belong.

Mindfulness for "Moroons"

Mindfulness can be defined in several different ways. Most simply it refers to a *clear and lucid awareness* of everyday experiences that is relatively free of the conceptualization and perceptual filters we so automatically place between ourselves and life. Mindfulness is an intensely focused, non-intrusive, non-judgmental awareness and acceptance of whatever IS at the moment. In other words, mindfulness means to PAY ATTENTION! Nothing more and nothing less.

In biblical imagery, mindfulness means we no longer cling to our graven images (concepts) of God or Reality. We look straight at IT, free of memories and regrets, hopes and expectations. We stop limiting our perception of Reality with words and just experience life. With sufficient practice, we will begin to realize that our everyday experience is sacred, that God speaks to us far more in the song of a solitary nightingale or the music of a mountain stream than in ten thousand sermons. Alan Watts put it this way.

> *Therefore, in the end we return to a truth that is both surprising and simple—namely, that our everyday experience is a spiritual experience of the highest order, that union with the Tao is not necessarily a strange state of consciousness nor a particular form of carefully regulated behavior. This truth, to be understood, must first be stood on its head and complicated; in other words, before we can once again feel our unity with the Tao, we must first feel the self-conscious separation from life, which is the peculiar characteristic of civilized man; before we can understand that nothing special has to be done to achieve it we have to go through the psychological process which I have described, undertaking the elusive and irritating task of chasing ourselves and falling into infinite regression through trying to combine things that were never separate. Unless this has been done, the mere statement that ordinary experience is a supreme spiritual experience will be meaningless.*[1]

The next time you eat an ice cream cone, try this little experiment. Focus on eating just that ice cream cone in just that moment. As you slurp away, don't compare it mentally to ice cream cones you have eaten in the past or wonder if there are more or better ice cream cones in your future. You have never eaten an ice cream cone before because the past no longer exists, except as ephemeral bytes of electrochemical energy stored somewhere in your cerebral cortex. And you will never eat another one because the future is yet to be, except in the vain imaginings of that same cortex. This is the only ice cream cone in existence. Well, at least it's the only one in your existence. So just eat the thing!

Feel the cold, sweet sensation on your tongue as the ice cream starts to melt and run down your throat. Swish it around in your mouth and feel the texture of it. Then with the next lick, experience all these same sensations as if you were tasting it for the very first time. Because you are. Every slurp—every moment—arising fresh and new and undefiled by fantasy, judgment, comparison, or plain inattention.

Then when it's gone, let it be gone. Don't mourn the ending of the experience or wonder wistfully for the rest of the day when you might be able to have another ice cream cone. Ice cream cones are like all other phenomena. They arise, they're here for awhile, and then they pass away. Don't cling to the experience (and if you do, notice that as well). Clinging is what causes most of our suffering (aversion comes in second). Go on to each subsequent experience unencumbered by such graven images of ice cream reality. Immerse yourself directly in the next moment and see how different life feels. Watch the knot in your psyche begin to unwind as you learn to be more in the present.

This is how to really eat an ice cream cone. This is also how to become more mindful on the spiritual journey. As a famous Zen master once said about life after enlightenment, "I chop wood! I carry water!" I guess they didn't have ice cream cones back then.

In his groundbreaking book, *Living Buddha, Living Christ*, Thich Nhat Hanh, the celebrated Vietnamese Buddhist monk, writes,

> *Mindfulness is the key. When you become aware of something, you begin to have enlightenment. When you drink a glass of water and are aware that you are drinking a glass of water deeply with your whole being, enlightenment is there in its initial form. To be enlightened is always to be enlightened about something. I am enlightened about the fact that I am drinking a glass of water. I can obtain joy, peace, and happiness just because of that enlightenment. When you look at the blue sky and are aware of it, the sky becomes real, and you become real. That is enlightenment, and enlightenment brings about true life and true happiness.[2]*

As we continue to practice lucid awareness of our surroundings and experiences in the present moment, we will begin to notice another important aspect of mindfulness. We will start to see the very subtle ways in which our minds and emotions operate.

While paying attention to the sensation of the ice cream as it caresses my tongue, for example, I may notice a thought creeping in from the fringes of my consciousness that reminds me that the ice cream cone is almost gone. Perhaps this thought is followed by a feeling of melancholy or regret that the experience will soon be over. Then this makes me think of the fact that all the enjoyable experiences of life, including life itself, are just fleeting moments—wisps of smoke that appear for a while and then disappear without a trace. In the space of three seconds, I have gone from eating ice cream to feeling profoundly depressed about the existential meaning of life. God, I need therapy!

Well, maybe not. It all depends on whether I have learned to observe these thoughts from a higher, more detached perspective or if I still identify with them as if they really belonged to that marvelous invention I call "me" and insist on riding them like a runaway train. As Stephen Levine writes so beautifully in *A Gradual Awakening*, his classic book on the practice of insight meditation,

> *An image about practicing meditation that may be helpful is that of standing at a railroad crossing, watching a freight train passing by. In each transparent boxcar, there is a thought. We try to look straight ahead into the present, but our attachments draw our attention into the contents of the passing boxcars: we identify with the various thoughts. As we attend to the train, we notice there's supper in one boxcar, but we just ate, so we're not pulled by that one. The laundry list is the next one, so we reflect for a moment on the blue towel hanging on the line to dry, but we wake up quite quickly to the present once again, as the next boxcar has someone in it meditating and we recall what we're doing. A few more boxcars go by with thoughts clearly recognized as thoughts. But, in the next one is a snarling*

lion chasing someone who looks like us. We stay with that one until it's way down the line to see if it got us. We identify with that one because it "means" something to us. We have an attachment to it. . . .

We stick to some and we don't stick to others. The train is just there—and the silent witness who's standing at the crossroads also seems to be there. Those are the first stages of trying to be mindful, trying to stay in the here and now.[3]

If I'm on a runaway train and don't know it, then that train is my only reality and I'm in big trouble. I can't get off because there's no "off" to get to. But when I finally realize I'm riding on an endless train of conditioned thoughts that constantly create painful experiences, I have taken my first steps on the path of mindfulness. And if I am learning to stand at the crossing, watching the cars go by and noticing what each contains without clinging to some or averting my gaze from others, then I am free. Or at least I'm beginning to taste freedom.

At this juncture you may be asking yourself the very reasonable question, "Why bother?" What's the point?" It obviously takes a lot of concentrated effort and attention to become mindful and aware. Most people don't know about it and, quite frankly, wouldn't try it if they did. If you insist on learning how to meditate and practice mindfulness in your daily life, you're probably going to stand out in a crowd. The more religiously conservative members of your family and circle of friends will likely become convinced that you have gone "Eastern" or "New Age" and begin placing your name on prayer lists all over the country. Your liberal friends will smile benevolently and figure it's a phase you will soon outgrow. After all, they did. So why even attempt this practice unless you just like being seen as odd? What could it possibly have to do with the spiritual journey?

Two years ago, Nancy and I decided to take the boys to see the Grand Canyon over spring break. None of us had been there before because, frankly, I could never see the point of traveling several hours to look at a big hole in the ground. I'd rather go to the ocean and get in touch with God. But Nancy finally prevailed (as she does on most things) and we started making plans. Since our friends, Bruce and Barbara, were Grand Canyon veterans many times over, we invited them to come along in our motor home as tour guides and companions. They foolishly agreed.

We left Riverside on a Thursday evening. I remember entering the park just as the sun was streaking the horizon. As I drove down the two-lane highway that runs across the high mesa leading to the rim, Bruce and Barbara awoke to tell me we were getting very close.

They told me to start watching out to the north. As we turned a corner a few minutes later, I saw a flash of red through the curtain of trees. Bruce whispered/hissed, "Stop! That's it!" Because I always do what Bruce tells me, I pulled to the side of the road and the three of us got out while Nancy and the boys continued to improvise musical riffs through their nostrils. As I stepped out into the morning air, I could smell the fragrance of the magnificent pine sentinels all around us. I immediately walked off by myself and crossed the fifty yards through the trees to the edge of the canyon rim.

There are no words. I've been sitting here at the computer for the past ten minutes trying to finish this story and that is the only thought that comes to mind. There are just no words to describe what I experienced that morning. Yes, I marveled at the morning shadows as they danced on red canyon walls that seemed to go on forever. And yes, I watched the Colorado River wend its way along the canyon floor like a silvery thread tossed to the ground by a giant seamstress. But there was something more. Something bigger. I was in the presence of a living thing. No, that's not it either.

I was in the presence of Life. I stood there peering over the precipice while the Canyon literally stole my breath away. I vaguely remember putting my hand to my heart as I looked across the broad expanse of space to the tree line on the North

Rim. I felt as if I were witnessing the beginning of the world. Tears streaked down my face before I even knew I was crying. It was like the first time I saw the ocean at the age of seventeen, only now I was forty-one.

Without so much as a warning, the Canyon had swallowed me up. I just disappeared into the Vastness of It. There was no longer anyone there to admire it or be in awe. There was only the Canyon. There was only God. And I knew I was being welcomed Home after a very long journey. I stood on the rim of eternity, captured by pure awareness, pure mindfulness. There was no more Richard Young with his quirky collection of hopes and dreams, fears and neuroses. All of that had been absorbed into stillness. There are simply no words.

We all have moments like this at one time or another in our lives—moments that give us a glimpse of a greater Reality, an all-encompassing consciousness of Unity. Such unexpected and profound experiences, whether of wonder or of pain, can creep up on us unawares and instantly dissolve the seemingly solid boundaries of our carefully constructed sense of identity. Most of us find this frightening, something akin to death or loss of control, and we turn away as quickly as possible (the average length of stay at the Grand Canyon is only thirty minutes). It is just too terrifying to feel so small and insignificant, so unreal. The good news is, such glimpses are quite fleeting. The bad news is, such glimpses are quite fleeting.

There are at least two things we need if we are ever to escape the painful illusion of separation that characterizes our normal state of consciousness and be "saved."

First, we need our religious institutions to "return to their first love" and remember that the permanent transformation of consciousness—not intellectual acceptance of theological doctrines and blind obedience to a set of ecclesiastical rules—is the highest goal of spiritual attainment. We must return to the spirit of Paul's admonition, "Be ye transformed by the renewing of your minds" (Rom. 12:2). Self-surrender or self-forgetfulness, which is the necessary precondition of Union with God, is always difficult and often frightening. We need all the individual and institutional encouragement and direction we can get.

Second, we need a spiritual methodology that has been proven effective in gradually eroding away the stony structure of our false and separative identity—because we can't afford to go to the Grand Canyon every day. The practice of mindfulness is just such a methodology. It has been used and taught by mystics and saints of every religious persuasion for at least five thousand years. There may be something to it.

What follows are a few short suggestions on how to become more mindful in your formal meditation and in your daily life. I encourage you to test them for yourself, as I did. If they don't work, toss 'em. If they do work, we'll row to the other side together.

"Can I Get a Witness?"

Human beings are born with the potential to be self-observant, to live life and simultaneously watch themselves living it. This ability is the foundation for human intuition and self-direction. It is also the basis for the development of mindfulness or sensitivity to the Holy Spirit. Here's how it works.

Rather than being completely identified with the experiences of our lives—constantly trying to avoid thoughts, feelings, and situations we fear or dislike and cling to those we desire—we learn to sit back, relax, and just watch the passing parade. We systematically develop an internal witness or "watcher within" who can remain detached from the mental and emotional roller coaster ride created by the aversions and desires of our separative ego-consciousness and simply observe whatever happens. We don't change it. We don't fix it. And we don't run from it. These things only invest life with the energy it needs to hurt us. We just sit still in our minds and watch. You see, a witness can't be harmed. It is totally imperturbable and completely safe. Feel the peace. You will be amazed at what begins to happen.

It is important that this witness self be free of judgment. Otherwise it becomes nothing more than self-consciousness or super-ego which has the power to block our free participation in the flow of life and cripple us emotionally. Sam Keen illustrates the inhibiting effects of such self-consciousness by telling the story of a centipede who tried to figure out how it walked and got so confused it tripped over its own legs. Add to this the fact the centipede had to spend several years in psychotherapy trying to cope with its shame and deep sense of inadequacy, and you're starting to get the picture.

Mindfulness must be free of all comparison and moral judgment. These are ego functions. They enable the ego to "exist" in its own imagination. Without them, we'd all be enlightened already. Therefore the internal witness must be objective and grace-full; it must observe all things with compassionate eyes that look for and find the Christ in every person and situation. The first rule of the witness is, "Judge not." Judgment presupposes comparison and identification—processes which render witnessing impossible. And one more thing. Invest your witness with a sense of humor. It helps.

Reconnect with Your Body

We all ride around in a body-shaped vehicle of relatively stable energy. Some people get a Mercedes and others of us have to settle for a Yugo. That aside, none of us should make the mistake of identifying too closely with this bag of bones. Sooner or later worms are going to eat it, and it will return to the earth from which it came. Thinking we are our bodies will only intensify our fears of life and death. But we shouldn't ignore our bodies either. They are intimately joined with our minds and are the means through which we touch the world. As such, they have much to teach us about the nature of Reality.

The previous chapter describes the first stages of formal meditation, when we learn to concentrate with a one-pointed awareness on some object, mantra, or experience. Such practice eventually enables us to focus intently and enter into profoundly peaceful modes of consciousness. But meditation should not end here. Once achieved, this concentrative ability should be turned toward the development of mindfulness and insight.

The easiest way to shift from the practice of concentration to mindfulness is to focus on the physical sensations of the body. Notice how your body feels. Be aware of any sensations in your arms and legs, in your back, shoulders, and neck. Don't be satisfied with easy conceptualizations like, "I feel pain," or "My back is stiff." Let yourself *move into* the sensation of pain or stiffness and be aware of its many component parts. Then observe how these numerous sensations arise and pass away, just like everything else in the manifest universe.

Welcome whatever sensations present themselves to your awareness, without clinging or aversion. Don't seek pleasant sensations or experiences and don't ignore painful ones. Push nothing away. Literally every feeling, every sensation is your teacher. Observe them objectively and dispassionately.

Then, when you rise from formal meditation, carry this practice into your daily life. Periodically throughout the day, remind yourself to sense your arms and legs for a few moments. Be openly aware of whatever sensations are there while you continue performing the task at hand. Mindfulness is not difficult. It is simply the opposite of being on automatic pilot. *Remembering* to be mindful is the problem. As you continue this practice over several months, you will begin to notice a remarkable increase in your perceptual clarity and emotional equanimity. Slowly but surely you will begin to awaken.

Slow Down a Little

Every action we undertake is made up of many different components. The simple act of picking up a coffee cup and taking a drink involves an incredibly complex series of neural impulses and subtle motions of which we are normally unaware. There would seem to be a part of our brain that can learn an action and place it in an automatic-performance mode very quickly and efficiently. This ability is quite useful in a world where everything moves at warp speed. We are rewarded for behaving unconsciously. The first commandment of the ego is, "Thou shalt not be aware!"

It is particularly difficult to remember to be mindful under such chaotic circumstances. So, slow down a little bit. Try performing simple tasks at very slow speeds and pay complete attention to the various sensations and nuances of the act. This is the philosophy behind such things as walking meditation and the Japanese tea ceremony. When we deliberately slow down our thoughts, words, and actions, our conscious minds can penetrate more deeply into the essence of the experience. You will soon find that any activity can be a meditation. You will also find that examining the inner workings of your daily experience can provide you with profound insights into the nature of your own mind.

Mindfulness is a simple practice aimed at increasing our spiritual sensitivity and insight into the nature of Reality. At the very least, it can help us to develop great equanimity in the face of adversity and tremendous love for all of creation. That alone would make it an indispensable spiritual discipline in these difficult times of racial genocide and ecological disaster. But mindfulness can also serve as the vehicle of our awakening. It is a reliable road to liberation that has been validated over thousands of years of usage in every religion and culture in the world.

No matter what our religious heritage or sectarian concerns, mindfulness can be profitably integrated into our spiritual journey. It is a way out of the pain of our separative consciousness because it gives us a glimpse of the deeper unity within every experience. It is a way to "come to ourselves and return to our Father's house." But don't take my word for it. Don't take anyone's word for it. Try it for yourself and see into the thing directly.

M EDITATION: *Self-Remembering*

The essence of mindfulness is to remain firmly rooted in a clear perception of the present moment. Such an awareness produces a tremendous feeling of peace and presence and connection. NOW is the only reality. We can only know the Truth in this moment . . . and this moment . . . and this moment.

There is no past and no future except in our imagination. But our minds tend to wander in these unrealities most of the time in order to give the ego a sense of ongoing existence. The price we pay for our inattention to the "Eternal Now" is pain and discomfort and a chronic sense of alienation from our own experience. Missing the moment keeps us in the "ego cramp" we have mistaken for our real selves.

It takes considerable discipline and practice to remain aware in the present moment. One of the best ways to begin is through a mindfulness technique developed years ago by G.I. Gurdjieff called "Self-Remembering." This exercise is based on the truth that the one thing that is inescapably a part of the present moment is our physical bodies. The body can't be in the past or in the future. It can only be right here, right now. It would follow, then, that focusing on the physical sensations of the body would enable us to remain aware and awake.

The exercise itself is incredibly simple. Just become aware of the feeling of your arms and legs. Do that right now. As you sit reading this book, feel your arms and legs. Be aware. Let your mind move out of your imagination and back into your body. What are you aware of? Do your arms and legs feel light or heavy? Are there any sensations that you would label as pain or discomfort? Do they feel good? Get up now and do something active for a few minutes, all the while remaining aware of your arms and legs. When you are finished, come back to this book and ask yourself the following questions:

> *What am I aware of while feeling my arms and legs?*
> *How does it affect my state of mind?*
> *How does it affect the actions I perform?*
> *How does this state of awareness compare to the times when*
> *I am not aware of my arms and legs?*

As you can see, this exercise is simple to perform. The difficulty arises in remembering to do it. Mindfulness is easy. Remembering to be mindful is not.

In his excellent book, *Living the Mindful Life*, Charles Tart suggests the use of various "alarm clocks" to help us remember to be awake to the present moment. For example, I might decide one morning that every time I put a key in a lock that day, I will feel my arms and legs for a few moments. Or I may choose to be mindful of my body every time I pick up a book or a piece of paper. Anything can serve as a reminder to be mindful: walking through doorways, getting into vehicles, eating, talking on the telephone, etc. The goal is to become so consistently mindful that we no longer need reminders.

Try this tomorrow at home or at work. Pick a mindfulness alarm clock that you encounter frequently during the day. Then resolve to be aware of your arms and legs for a minute or two every time you encounter that signal. At the end of the day, evaluate your experience of increased mindfulness.

If it seems to be of any value, repeat the exercise the following day using a different signal (since the mind tends to habituate to stimuli so quickly). See if mindfulness changes anything. Prove it to yourself!

10

STATIONS OF THE CROSS

You are greatly mistaken if you look for anything save to endure trials, for all this mortal life is full of troubles, and everywhere marked with crosses. The further a man advances in the spiritual life, the heavier and more numerous he finds the crosses, for his ever-deepening love of God makes more bitter the sorrows of his earthly life.

THOMAS À KEMPIS

We are called to be other Christs ourselves. Yet to hear the call to be other Christs, we must be awakened. Jesus is an awakener. The awakening he brings is essential because so many of us are asleep and as good as dead. It is Jesus who raises from the dead, who arouses us from our slumber, who awakens and excites to new life.

MATTHEW FOX

THE STATIONS of the Cross have been a poignant part of Catholic liturgy and tradition for centuries. Being a good Protestant boy, I was completely ignorant of their liturgical significance as well as their deeper pathos and beauty.

My ignorance was unassailed until I began to lead yearly meditation retreats with my friend and colleague, Bruce

Langford, at St. Andrew's Abbey, a Benedictine monastery located in the foothills outside Valyermo, California. Spread across the hillside behind this wonderful monastery are fifteen life-sized crosses with abstract sculptures attached which symbolize the various phases of Christ's journey of death, burial, and resurrection. I have walked these stations many times on my numerous trips to the monastery. At first, I was curious and intrigued—an open-minded student of Catholicism. Then I was interested in ways to integrate the stations with my own spiritual journey. Finally, I was embraced by their mystery.

Bruce and I wrote and compiled the following commentaries and stories for use on one of our meditation retreats at St. Andrew's. We walked together in silence as a community of faith through the stations and heard each of these read aloud. As you read them, be mindful of the truth that these stations are meant to symbolize the various experiences and phases of our own spiritual development. Each of us in our own way must journey to Golgotha, the place of the skull, and suffer the pain and fear of self-surrender. Only then can we lay aside our befuddled egos and be resurrected to a new perception of ourselves, of one another, and of God. Herein lies the end of pain and separation and the beginning of liberation.

Station One: Jesus Condemned

For many of us, the spiritual journey begins after some tragedy or great disappointment. We lose our job or decide to divorce our spouse. A loved one becomes gravely ill or dies. And our ego project begins to show the stress fractures of life's constant tremors. We feel mocked by our apparent powerlessness over the circumstances of our lives. Like Jesus, we are seemingly judged and condemned by other people and external events.

What we can't yet know is that condemnation always begins as an internal process that we then project onto the world. We are literally being wounded by our own ego, which consigns us to a life of pain and guilt by its stubborn insistence on the reality of separation. But after we have tried every other approach, the pain may force us to look deeper within ourselves to understand and eventually dispel the ego-illusion that imprisons us. This is the true beginning of spiritual practice when, like the Prodigal, we "come to ourselves" and take the first faltering steps towards Home. Consider this story:

> *A lion was taken into captivity and thrown into a concentration camp where, to his amazement, he found other lions who had been there for years, some of them all their lives, for they had been born there. He soon became acquainted with the social activities of the camp lions. They banded themselves into groups. One group consisted of the socializers; another was into show business; another was cultural, for its purpose was to carefully preserve the customs, the tradition, and the history of the times when lions were free; other groups were religious— they gathered mostly to sing moving songs about a future jungle where there would be no fences; some groups attracted those who were literary and artistic by nature; others still were revolutionary, and they met to plot against their captors or against other revolutionary groups. Every now and then a revolution would break out, one particular group would be wiped out by another, or the guards would all be killed and replaced by another set of guards.*
>
> *As he looked around, the newcomer observed one lion who always seemed deep in thought, a loner who belonged to no group and mostly kept away from everyone. There was something strange about him that commanded everyone's admiration and everyone's hostility, for his presence aroused fear and self-doubt. He said to the newcomer, "Join no group. These poor fools are busy with everything except what is essential."*
>
> *"And what is that?" asked the newcomer.*
>
> *"Studying the nature of the fence."*[1]

Station Two: Jesus Given the Cross

Once the decision is made to begin the journey back to our original identity, we have only to choose a Path—to pick up one cross or another. Each one comes with its own rewards and its own price. But, in Truth, it matters less which cross we carry than *how* we carry it.

If we carry our cross the way the world does—mindlessly and unaware—we will travel in a perpetual circle, frequently exchanging one cross for another as we search in vain for the "right one" or at least an easier one. Over the years our cross will grow heavier with the weight of our illusions, and we will grow more angry and confused each time we stumble and fall. To move skillfully through this world, we must become increasingly more mindful as illustrated by this story:

> *When a guest volunteered to do the dishes after dinner the Master said, "Are you sure you know how to do dishes?"*
>
> *The man protested that he had done them all his life. Said the Master: "Ah, I have no doubt of your ability to make dishes clean—I only doubt your ability to wash them."*
>
> *This is the explanation he gave his disciples later: "There are two ways to wash dishes: one is to wash them in order to make them clean; the other is to wash them in order to wash them."*
>
> *That was still far from clear, so he added: "The first action is dead because while your body does the dishes your mind is fixed on the goal of cleaning them; the second is alive because your mind is where your body is."* [2]

Spiritual discernment begins when we embrace the Path we have chosen and walk it with mindfulness and attention. The way to bear a cross is to *feel* the full weight of it. That is the beginning of straightening the Path and moving toward Home.

Station Three: Jesus' First Fall

The exhilaration of beginning the journey is always . . . always followed by a fall. There is no escaping it. Contrary to popular belief and most religious teaching, it is absolutely impossible to live life only on the positive side of the ledger. Not even Christ could do it. Besides, a journey without misfortune is no journey at all. In order to appreciate the exhilaration of riding the crest of a wave, we must first spend time being churned in the cloudy waters of the trough. A ship is safe in the harbor. But a ship is not built for the harbor.

How do we react that first time we fall? Do we despair? Turn back? Ignore the help offered by others? Cry "Abba, Father, I knew this wouldn't work"? Or do we pick up our cross, return to our Path, place one foot in front of the other, and—for no other reason than because we have chosen to do so—move slowly toward the faint sound of our Father's voice?

> *Once upon a time a traveler was lost in the desert and despaired of ever finding water. He struggled up one hilltop then another and another in the hope of sighting a stream somewhere. He kept looking in every direction with no success.*
>
> *As he staggered onward, his foot caught on a dry bush and he stumbled to the ground. That's where he lay, with no energy even to rise, no desire to struggle anymore, no hope of surviving this ordeal.*
>
> *As he lay there, helpless and dejected, he suddenly became aware of the silence of the desert. On all sides a majestic stillness reigned, undisturbed by the slightest sound. Suddenly he raised his head. He had heard something. Something so faint that only the sharpest ear and the deepest silence would lead to its detection: the sound of running water.*
>
> *Heartened by the hope that the sound aroused in him, he rose and kept moving till he arrived at a stream of fresh, cool water.*[3]

Station Four: Jesus Meets His Mother

The Path of Awakening is always an inward journey to the very depths of the Mind. It is, to a large extent, a solitary passage that requires Odyssean strength and courage if we are ever to return to our true home in the transformed consciousness of Union. We cannot look to fate or circumstance or other people to ease our burden or direct our steps. We must literally become our own teacher—so much so that if we see Buddha or Christ on the road, we are directed to kill him! Neither Buddha nor Christ nor Gandhi nor any other traveler can take the journey for us. We must go it alone.

But the moment we pick ourselves up from the fall and resolve to go on no matter what, we encounter a vast internal reservoir of spiritual sustenance, a previously undiscovered sea of life-giving energy. It is a profound mystery of the spiritual life that when we abandon all hope of external help, we are embraced by the Mother within us and nurtured by the wisdom of our own hearts. As the Buddha once said, "Be a lamp to yourself. Be your own confidence. Hold to the truth within yourself, as to the only truth."

A devotee once knelt to be initiated into discipleship. The guru whispered the sacred mantra into his ear, warning him not to reveal it to anyone.

"What will happen if I do?" asked the devotee.

Said the guru, "Anyone you reveal the mantra to will be liberated from the bondage of ignorance and suffering, but you yourself will be excluded from discipleship and suffer damnation."

No sooner had he heard those words, than the devotee rushed to the marketplace, collected a large crowd around him, and repeated the sacred mantra for all to hear.

The disciples later reported this to the guru and demanded that the man be expelled from the monastery for his disobedience.

The guru smiled and said, "He has no need of anything I can teach. His action has shown him to be a guru in his own right."[4]

Station Five: Simon Helps Jesus

Even as we marvel at our new-found center of strength and peace, we must take care how we celebrate the victory. Every advance on the Prodigal Journey can and will be used by the ego to delay further development. Self-reliance is no exception. Once we learn to depend upon our own internal resources rather than always looking to others for help, the ego begins to create and refine a very subtle form of spiritual pride. It will try to convince us we don't need anyone and that no one can do this journey as well as we can. This only serves to reinforce the primary dualism of self and other. Spiritual determination and taking responsibility for our choices are one thing. Egoism is quite another. Of course, we can't really blame the ego for trying. It knows where this journey is leading.

How many times have we been offered a helping and loving hand only to turn it aside with "No thanks, I must do this myself?" There is no weakness or shame in taking hold of the proffered hand of someone further along or accepting a gentle push from someone just behind. Besides, it only looks as though we are traveling single-file. We are really all moving in parallel.

There was once a very austere man who let no food or drink pass his lips while the sun was in the heavens. In what seemed to be a sign of heavenly approval for his austerities, a bright star shone on top of a nearby mountain, visible to everyone in broad daylight, though no one knew what had brought the star there.

One day the man decided to climb the mountain. A little village girl insisted on going with him. The day was warm and soon the two were thirsty. He urged the child to drink but she said she would not unless he drank too. The poor man was in a quandary. He hated to break his fast; but he hated to see the child suffer from thirst. Finally, he drank. And the child with him.

For a long time he dared not to look up to the sky, for he feared the star had gone. So imagine his surprise when, on looking up after a while, he saw two stars shining brightly above the mountain. [5]

Station Six: Veronica Wipes Jesus' Face

We no longer experience reality directly. We understand only what we can describe in language or represent with logical ideas. We have mistaken our verbal images of reality for Reality itself—like mistaking the map for the territory. Language and logic rend the seamless fabric of reality by making endless distinctions between "this and that." We are like the owner of a vast kingdom who, for no apparent reason, became frightened of his neighbors and went to live in a small, fortified corner of his land. After many years of telling himself that this was the only safe place, he forgot all about his mansions, his servants, and his formal gardens. He then passed this tiny plot of land on to his children and never told them of all he had left behind.

Language and logic, the very essence of the discursive intellect, inflame our fear and hide the truth of our identity. They can never lead us to a knowledge of our true estate.

Awareness and intuition, the nonrational and holistic powers of our mind, are the "Royal Road" to direct revelation from our own divine center. When our eyes become clouded by the language and logic of the ego, intuition gently wipes our face and clears our vision so we can once again see the Way to our Father's house.

> *The Master always taught that Truth was right before our eyes and the reason we did not see it was our lack of perspective.*
>
> *Once he took a disciple on a mountain trip. When they were halfway up the mountain the man glared at the underbrush and complained, "Where's the beautiful scenery you are always talking about?"*
>
> *The Master grinned. "You're standing on top of it as you will see when we reach the peak."*[6]

Station Seven: Jesus' Second Fall

We feared it was coming. It was probably inevitable. That moment when the steady constancy of pain is accented by the searing jolt of another fall. Knees and elbows meet the pavement. Flesh scrapes from the bone. Gravel embedded in both hands.

We dared to hope that the worst pain was over. We thought we were finally getting it right. We thought we were going Home. Is this the reward we get for pressing on and refusing to give up? Maybe the price of this cross is too high. Letting go of the ego is just too much to ask of anyone, isn't it? Is there another cross that might be easier to bear? Can't we just stay down this time? We know standing back up probably means falling again . . . and again . . . and again.

What was that about self-reliance and intuitive wisdom? Such metaphysical babel does little to answer our desperate questions. How do we stop the hurting? How do we get away? Do we really need this intense pain in order to return Home?

> *There is a story that is told of a maharaja who went out to sea when a great storm arose. One of the slaves on board began to cry out and wail in fear, for the man had never been on a ship before. His crying was so loud and so prolonged that everyone on board began to be annoyed and the maharaja was for throwing the man overboard.*
>
> *But his chief advisor, who was a sage, said, "No. Let me deal with the man. I think I can cure him."*
>
> *With that he ordered some of the sailors to hurl the man into the sea. The moment he found himself in the sea the poor slave began to scream in terror and to thrash out wildly. In a few seconds the sage ordered him to be hauled on board.*
>
> *Back on board the slave lay in a corner in absolute silence. When the maharaja asked his advisor for the reason, he replied, "We never realize how lucky we are till our situation gets worse."[7]*

Maybe the answers are not found in crying out or running away. Maybe the way to avoid repeating THIS pain is to experience it once and for all, to let it sweep over us like a wave and note its passing. Did Jesus seek to escape the pain or did He embrace it? There in the dust—right over there—what was He thinking?

Station Eight: Women Mourn Jesus

As our meditation and mindfulness deepen, we will experience partial glimpses of Reality. As we become increasingly more detached from the things of this world and more aware of the subtle workings of our own ego, the inner eye of our heart flickers open to show us our true nature. These glimpses can take many forms, like feeling our self disappear into a sunset or being temporarily overcome with love for a group of complete strangers. Such experiences of "direct seeing" are themselves revelatory and transformative and are sources of great spiritual comfort.

But this intuitive process of opening and awareness is not always peaceful or consoling. It is often disturbing to the ego because it marks the eventual surrender of our limited ego-sense, which is always subjectively experienced as a kind of death. The women of Jerusalem, our own intuitive powers, mourn because they understand the end of the ego is near. As Paul Brunton once wrote,

> *Be still and know! This is to be done by practising the art of meditation deeply and then—for it cannot properly be done before—tracing the ego to its hidden lair. Here it must be faced. Being still involves the achievement of mental silence, without which the ego remains cunningly active and keeps us within its sphere of influence. Knowing involves penetrating to the ego's secret source where, in its lulled and weakened condition, it can be confronted and killed.*
>
> *The ego knows that if profoundly concentrated attention is directed toward ascertaining its true nature the result will be suicidal, for its own illusory nature would be revealed. This is why it opposes such a meditation and why it allows all other kinds.*[8]

Our fear of the unknown and our terror of death are the ego's final trump cards. They are the angels with flaming swords that guard the entrance back into the Garden. We must not turn back now. We must say along with Christ, "Women of Jerusalem, do not weep for me!"

Station Nine: Jesus' Third Fall

Neither our worst nightmares nor our most morbid imaginings could have prepared us for this barren wilderness. All of life becomes arid and dry. Where is God? Where is life or love or even faint hope? The emptiness of this spiritual desert is made worse because we dared to believe we were moving closer. Here, in the dirt, it seems we are further from Home than ever before. From this point on, we must proceed in darkness.

In the middle of this screaming crowd, it is so still, so empty. We would run, but this place is directionless—devoid of anything familiar. No, that's not right. It's all very familiar, but it no longer means anything. All the things that used to bring us comfort on this journey—our hopes, our dreams, even our aspirations for finding God—they have all turned to dust that parches our throats. There is no balm in Gilead.

Have we gone blind or is there just nothing to see? There is nowhere else. Everywhere is this place. What we most need in this dark journey is an unfaltering trust in the Divine guidance as well as the courage to risk everything. As Thomas Merton writes,

> *Do you think your meditation has failed? On the contrary: this bafflement, this darkness, this anguish of helpless desire is a fulfillment of meditation. For if meditation aims above all at establishing in your soul a vital contact of love with the living God, then as long as it only produces images and ideas and affections that you can understand, feel and appreciate, it is not yet done its full quota of work. But when it gets beyond the level of your understanding and your imagination, it is really bringing you close to God, for it introduces you into the darkness where you can no longer think of Him, and are consequently forced to reach out for Him by blind faith and hope and love.*[9]

Every great mystic and dedicated contemplative has experienced this "Dark Night of the Soul," a place seemingly abandoned by the Divine, steeped in utter stagnation. The emptiness is so complete there is not even room for despair. The only solace may be this: Jesus walked this way.

Station Ten: Jesus Stripped

Just as Jesus was stripped of all his clothes, we must be stripped of all our attachments. Grasping after what we must possess and avoiding what we cannot abide is how we create our greatest suffering.

By this point in the journey, we have become detached from most of what the world loves and hates. We have learned to accept the flow of experience with equanimity and to observe it with mindfulness. We can finally ride and swim with the strong current of the Tao. But now we must detach ourselves from the very desire that has brought us to this point—our desire for God. We must be completely naked in order to enter into the Holy or Holies; naked of all desire, all aversion, and all vain imaginings about transformation and freedom. We must become like vessels that have been emptied of water so they may be filled with wine. Or like glass, cleansed of all dust and grime, so we may receive the sun and vanish into its light.

Anand was Buddha's most devoted disciple. Years after Buddha's death a Great Council of the Enlightened was planned and one of the disciples went to tell Anand about it.

Now at the time Anand was still not enlightened himself though he had worked at it strenuously for years. So he was not entitled to attend the council.

On the evening of the council meeting he was still not enlightened so he determined to practice vigorously all night and not stop till he had attained his goal. But all he succeeded in doing was making himself exhausted. He had not made the slightest progress in spite of all his efforts.

So toward dawn he decided to give up and get some rest. In

that state in which he had lost all greed, even for enlighten-
ment, he rested his head on the pillow. And he suddenly be-
came enlightened![10]

Station Eleven: Jesus Nailed

The complete surrender of our finite and separate ego is very
near. We have learned to free ourselves from the twin demons
of grasping and avoidance. Everything is accepted, nothing is
pushed away. The Prodigal is almost Home. As the following
story illustrates, we will find that our journey towards self-surrender frightens some and inspires others.

In a concentration camp there lived a prisoner who, even
though he was under sentence of execution, was fearless and
free. One day he was seen in the middle of the prison square
playing a guitar. A large crowd gathered to listen, for under the
spell of the music, they became as fearless as he. When the
prison authorities saw this, they forbade the man to play.

But the next day there he was again, singing and playing on
his guitar with a larger crowd around him. The guards angrily
dragged him away and had his fingers chopped off.

Next day he was back, singing and making what music he
could with his bleeding fingers. This time the crowds were
cheering. The guards dragged him away again and smashed his
guitar.

The following day he was singing with all his heart. What
a song! So pure and uplifting! The crowd joined in, and while
the singing lasted, their hearts became as pure as his and their
spirits as invincible. So angry were the guards this time that
they had his tongue torn out. A hush descended on the camp,
a something that was deathless.

To the astonishment of everyone, he was back at his place
the next day swaying and dancing to a silent music that no one
but he could hear. And soon everyone was holding hands and
dancing around this bleeding, broken figure in the center while
the guards stood rooted to the ground in wonder.[11]

There is still some pain at this stage of the journey, as when the nails join us to the cross, but there is no suffering. Suffering cannot exist where desire and aversion have been transcended. And the cross—our spiritual Path—which once seemed like such a burden, is now bearing us on *its* back. We can even feel it lifting us up toward heaven.

Station Twelve: Jesus Dies

Every mystic must wander in the wilderness of the Dark Night of the Soul and then "die" to his or her limited perception of this world. This sacrificial death is on a higher plane than mere virtue or practiced discipline. Here the Cross of Christ enters fully into the life of the contemplative. Without the mystical death that completely separates us from created things, there is no perfect freedom and no advance into the promised land of mystical union.

When the ego finally dies to itself and is transformed, there is no more need for discipline or choices or self-reliance. We can finally throw off the terrible duty of our own salvation. We no longer have to walk the dusty back roads of the journey on our own power or agonize alone in the garden—we *are* the journey . . . and the back roads . . . and the garden . . . and the cross. We are finally NOTHING—NO/THING. And in so being, we are Everything and All.

> *Tajima no Kami was fencing master to the Shogun.*
>
> *One of the Shogun's bodyguards came to him one day asking to be trained in swordsmanship.*
>
> *"I have watched you carefully," said Tajima no Kami, "and you seem to be a master in the art yourself. Before taking you on as a pupil, I request you to tell me what master you studied under."*
>
> *The bodyguard replied, "I have never studied the art under anyone."*
>
> *"You cannot fool me," said the teacher. "I have a discerning eye and it never fails."*

"*I do not mean to contradict your excellency,*" *said the guard, "but I really do not know a thing about fencing."*

The teacher engaged the man in swordplay for a few minutes then stopped and said, "Since you say you have never learned the art, I take your word for it. But you are some kind of master. Tell me about yourself."

"There is one thing," said the guard. "When I was a child I was told by a samurai that a man should never fear death. I therefore struggled with the question of death till it ceased to cause me the slightest anxiety."

"So that's what it is," cried Tajima no Kami. "The ultimate secret of swordsmanship lies in being free from the fear of death. You need no training. You are a master in your own right."[12]

Station Thirteen: Jesus Taken Down

When the practice of mindfulness leads us finally to see through and surrender our separative and fearful ego-sense, we no longer need the cross. Gone is the time when we are required to bear the weight of our journey as a burden upon our hearts—sometimes exciting, sometimes painful, always challenging. Gone too is the time when the journey seems to carry us along effortlessly and then lift us up to the highest heaven. Once we are "crucified with Christ," we have no further need for the structured illusion of the spiritual journey. Quite simply, there is no one left to go on such a quest. Jesus—who symbolizes the personal psyche or persona with which we have always been identified—has been "taken down" from his place of temporary ascendancy to make room for the Christ. Alan Watts wrote this about the state of absolute self-less-ness:

What are you to do, or not do? The dilemma that you thought was you is simply not there at all. Now, do not make it difficult. That is a form of evading it. Do not make it easy. That is a form of evading it. It is neither difficult nor easy, because if it were difficult, it would have to be difficult for someone. If it

*were easy, it would have to be easy for someone, and the some-
one we are talking about is just the one that is not there. If you
think it is there, okay, you can have that thought—but it is a
thought. In other words, your ego is a thought among thoughts.
It is not the controlling thinker, or the feeler, or the sensor. It is
this thing that is going along, and we get anxious because we
feel nobody is in control. But nobody ever was.*[13]

Station Fourteen: Jesus Entombed

The old dualistic sense of self is now symbolically entombed.
That is, the ego-thought goes back into the "Ground of all Being" from whence it came—there to be transformed and reunited with all Life. As the Christ once said, "A seed must first
go into the ground and die if it is to bear much fruit." Here is
the end of all dualisms between self and other and between life
and death. The fixed gulf that appears to separate "sinful" humanity from a righteous God is not bridged by a supernatural
act of infanticide. We simply come to see that the gulf has never
existed, that we are one with God, that the individual soul or
Atman is one with Brahman, or God. It could be no other way.
This is how the Hermetic writers of the third century spoke of
this same truth:

*If you don't make yourself equal to God, you can't perceive
God; for like is known by like. Leap free of everything that is
physical, and grow as vast as that immeasurable vastness; step
beyond all time and become eternal; then you will perceive
God. Realize that nothing is impossible for you; recognize that
you too are immortal and that you can embrace all things in
your mind; find your home in the heart of every living creature;
make yourself higher than all heights and lower than all
depths; bring all opposites inside yourself and reconcile them;
understand that you are everywhere, on the land, in the sea, in
the sky; realize that you haven't yet been begotten, that you are
still in the womb, that you are young, that you are old, that you
are dead, that you are in the world beyond the grave; hold all*

this in your mind, all times and places, all substances and qualities and magnitudes; then you can perceive God.[14]

Station Fifteen: God Raises Jesus

The Prodigal's "Journey of Return" is now complete. Jesus has awakened to his true identity as God's Son, the creative Logos of the universe. No longer can he be tormented by his own dark illusions of reality. No more shall his awareness be trapped in a self-made prison of finite space and limited time. The nightmare of separation is over and he who was lost has been found. He shall abide now and forever within the arms of Infinite Peace and Eternal Love. And so shall we all.

> *Once upon a time a little black boy was watching the balloon man at the Country Fair. The man was evidently a good salesman, because he allowed a red balloon to break loose and soar high up in the air, thereby attracting a crowd of prospective young customers.*
>
> *Next he released a blue balloon, then a yellow one, and a white one. They all went soaring up into the sky until they disappeared. The little black boy stood looking at the black balloon for a long time, then asked, "Sir, if you sent the black one up, would it go as high as the others?"*
>
> *The balloon man gave the kid an understanding smile. He snapped the string that held the black balloon in place and, as it soared upward, said, "It isn't the color, son. It's what's inside that makes it rise."*[15]

Jesus' death, burial, and resurrection symbolize the stages of his spiritual Realization: the gradual detachment from ego, the mindful descent into the inner depths of the mind, and the glorious awakening to Reality. His completion of this journey has awakened him to his complete Unity and Oneness within the Godhead, as the Christ. Now he joins all the other Avatars of history to share with us his transformed consciousness of Reality. In him, we shall all rise!

11

LOVING-KINDNESS

If I speak with the tongues of men and of angels, but do not have love, I have become a noisy gong or a clanging cymbal.

St. Paul

All the major religious traditions claim that the acid test of any spirituality is the degree to which it has been integrated into daily life. As the Buddha said, after enlightenment one should "return to the marketplace" and practice compassion for all living beings. A sense of peace, serenity, and loving-kindness are the hallmarks of all true religious insight.

Karen Armstrong

I ONCE knew a little boy who had a very difficult time adjusting to life in the first grade. He was a good kid who usually loved going to school. He couldn't wait to learn how to read and write. But for some reason, he hated being in the first grade. He was tall for his age and very bright and inquisitive, if somewhat shy. His father was a salesman for a small chain of appliance stores and his mother was a homemaker. He had one brother who was three years younger and a teenaged uncle who lived with the family. He had completed a very successful year in kindergarten learning the intricacies of finger painting, afternoon naps, and chasing girls on the playground. He had made an excellent transition to the school environment and related well to his teacher and peers. This made it difficult to understand why he was having trouble in the first grade. Here is his story as nearly as I can remember.

The Hershey Man

During the summer following kindergarten, the little boy's father was transferred to a different appliance store and was forced to relocate his family to another city. Due to financial problems, his parents rented a small, three-bedroom house on the east side of town in a poor area inhabited primarily by African-American families. This was during the early Sixties and racial tension was just beginning to build throughout the country. In this particular city, Black families were forced by various forms of economic discrimination to live in this poor and largely segregated area.

The little boy's new home seemed strange and a little frightening. He had always lived in white, middle-class neighborhoods and had never really interacted with Black people. He was completely ignorant of the increasing fragility of race relations at that time in our nation's history. He was an innocent-at-large. He had no experience with prejudice or racism because his parents tried to accept people's differences and had raised him to be tolerant of others as well. He was just a little boy living in a new town, hoping to find some new friends.

As September approached, the little boy became less frightened and more excited about going back to school. Most of all, he was excited about learning how to read books without the help of his mother or uncle. He had dozens of story books in his collection. His mother almost always let him buy a new Golden Book at the Safeway store whenever she went grocery shopping. He loved his books and was always very careful to keep them stacked neatly in his bedroom closet, well away from his little brother's smaller stack. He had each book completely memorized and could recite them rapidly and flawlessly to whomever cared to listen—or not. But that wasn't the same as reading and the little boy knew it. He longed to be able to read the big fat books on his parents' bookshelf without anyone having to read it to him first.

On the first day of classes at Whittier Elementary School, the little boy's father walked with him the few blocks between their house and the school so he would be sure to know his way home that afternoon. When they reached the playground, the little boy tried to be patient while his father ran through the universal parental checklist of "First Day of School" instructions for the twentieth time. "Now make sure you walk straight home after school, pal, so mom doesn't worry about you."

"Yes, daddy, I will."

"It should only take you about twenty minutes."

"I know, daddy."

"And don't stop to buy candy on the way home either."

"I won't, okay!"

"Do you have your lunch?"

"Yes, daddy. Can I go now?"

His dad patted him affectionately on the head and gave him an encouraging smile. The little boy waved as his father turned to walk away. He felt excited and a little scared, but he was determined to be brave on his first day of school. He glanced down at his brand new sneakers for reassurance and headed across the schoolyard towards the huge, four-story brick building. What he couldn't know was that his father was watching his progress through worried eyes from behind a nearby tree. The little boy also didn't notice that about 80% of the children on the playground were Black. He didn't notice because he was still "color blind." All he saw was a bunch of kids he didn't know, playing together and having fun. He wanted to have fun, too.

During the first recess that day, the little boy walked around the playground eagerly looking for someone to play with or something to do. Because of his love of sports, he gravitated naturally towards the baseball diamond where fifth- and sixth-graders were playing ball. When he said something about joining them, they laughed at him. Then they quickly and gleefully educated him to the fact that little baby first-graders were not welcome at their diamond, and he had better haul his butt out of there right now!

The little boy was hurt and almost started to cry. He didn't know there were rules against first-graders playing baseball. Why did big boys always have to be so mean to little kids anyway? As he turned to leave, he noticed a huge sixth-grade boy with coal-black skin standing quietly behind the backstop and looking for all the world like he was the boss of the playground. He must have weighed 300 pounds. Besides his immense size, his most distinguishing characteristic was the fact that he had several chocolate bars shoved into the breast pocket of his shirt even while he munched on another one. Apparently this was how he maintained his sizable girth. The little boy heard someone yell, "Hey Hershey Man, give me one of your candy bars!"

He answered in a laconic voice that was as deep as any man's. "You know better than to ask me for a candy bar, man. Nobody ever eats these but me, and don't you forget it or I'll have to come over there and give you a little reminder." The little boy thought it odd that the Hershey Man's words sounded mean even though his voice was smiling.

Later that same week, the little boy was still wandering the playground forlornly, searching for a friend. Nobody seemed to care that he was new in town and very lonely. Whenever he walked near the marble games being played in the dirt or the monkey bars, the kids ignored him. He just wanted to play with someone. He didn't even care what game they were playing as long as he could join in. He hated being alone.

One day during lunch recess, a tall black girl suddenly appeared standing right in front of him. He was pretty sure he had never seen her before. She looked big enough to be a sixth-grader. Her hair was done up in pigtails all over her head and she had a dark gap where one of her front teeth belonged. He looked up at her expectantly, hoping she might want to be his friend. Just as he was about to smile, she slapped him in the face with her open hand so hard he fell to the ground.

The little boy was so stunned he couldn't cry for several seconds. All the air was knocked from his lungs, and he felt as if his entire body had been thrown to the ground by a huge electrical current applied suddenly to his left cheek. He sat there dazed, with tears leaking down his face, trying vainly to catch his breath and unable to understand what had just happened or why. The unpredictability of this encounter with pain was far more frightening to the little boy than the pain itself.

He looked up at the girl, hoping for some sign that would help him interpret the meaning of this event so he could make sure it never happened again. He saw what he would one day understand was a child's face made old by the undeserved hatred she had already received in her life. But at that moment, all he could see through his tears was the ugliness and disgust she spewed in his direction. "Don't you ever look at me again, you worthless piece of white honkey shit. And stay out of my way because the next time I see you I'm gonna use my fist instead of the palm of my hand!"

When it looked as if she might strike him again, the little boy jumped up and ran towards the school so he could hide in one of the many stairwells inside. When he reached the back door of the building, he remembered he was not allowed to go in until after he heard the bell ring. He didn't want to get in trouble so he crouched in a corner behind the big stone steps of Whittier Elementary School and cried as if his heart would break. There was an autumn chill in the air.

The little boy spent the next several weeks hiding from the tall girl with the pigtails. Whenever he saw someone on the playground who looked anything like her, he would either run as fast as he could for his hiding place behind the old stone steps or go over and stay near the yard-duty teacher. He didn't feel he could tell anyone what had happened. His father was always at work, his mother was always busy cleaning the house, and his teacher didn't like tattletales. Besides, if he told on her, the tall girl would probably just beat him up again after school. So the little boy lived in frightened silence and kept to himself.

And in the midst of his self-imposed isolation, he became increasingly unhappy.

One day something happened that made the little boy feel very good. His teacher gave everyone in the class their own copy of the first "Dick and Jane" book. It wasn't quite as fat as the ones in his parents' bookcase, but it was much more substantial than any of his story books. He loved everything about this book, from the way it felt heavy in his hand, to the texture of the pages, to the smell of the binding. He couldn't believe his good fortune. His first real book! Of course it wasn't really his book, but he could pretend it was for a while. The teacher even said they could take them home to read! The little boy couldn't wait to show it to his parents and read the words he had already learned.

The next morning, he arrived at school a little earlier than usual with his precious book tucked safely under his arm. He sat down in the swings near the baseball diamond so he could leaf through the pages and enjoy the words and pictures once more. He was there only a couple of minutes when, out of the corner of his eye, he caught a glimpse of a girl with pigtails moving towards him on the left. Without looking in her direction, he slammed the book shut, grabbed it tightly in his right hand, and started running as if his life depended on it. Even before he reached the backstop, he could hear her cruel laughter and taunting words as her longer legs quickly closed the gap between them. "You'll never get away from me, Whitey. Come here and let me teach you some respect!"

The little boy kept running and dodging like a fullback breaking through the defensive line of an opposing team. But no matter how fast he ran or how quickly he cut, he could not elude her. With every ragged breath he took, he could hear her pounding footsteps getting closer. Suddenly she lunged forward and pushed him hard. He fell in a heap, scraping his hands in the dirt and pebbles near the pitcher's mound and dropping the book just out of his reach. As he looked down at the trickles of blood on his hands, tears began to form once more in his eyes. The tall, black girl with the missing tooth snatched up his book and said, "You don't need this. You're too stupid to read." Then she grabbed it roughly by its cover and flung it as hard as she could into the wind. The pages opened up and rustled loudly as if the book were trying to spread its wings and fly. But it fell to earth like a stone, landing open-faced in the dirt behind home plate.

A deep voice called out from behind the backstop, "Hey Trisha, leave the little white kid alone."

"Why don't you just kiss my black butt, Maarrvvvinnn?"

The voice got even deeper, "I said, leave him alone."

The tall girl looked at the backstop with contempt in her eyes. Then she turned slowly and walked back to a group of girls who had been watching and cheering her from the sidelines. As the little boy started brushing the dirt from his hands, the Hershey Man ambled over and handed him the book that had just been launched into space. The cover was bent and the pages were a little wrinkled and dirty but it wasn't much the worse for wear. The Hershey Man reached down and helped the little boy to his feet. "Do you know anything about baseball?" he asked in his slow, molasses-smooth voice.

"I can already throw the ball and my dad is teaching me how to hit," the little boy replied eagerly, hardly noticing the stinging pain in his hands.

"Good. You meet us out here at the first recess, boy, and we'll see how good you really are."

When the bell rang for school to begin, the big black boy and the little white boy walked together towards the building, laughing and talking all the way. The other kids watched them as they walked by because they seemed such an unlikely pair. As they were about to enter the back door, the Hershey Man reached into his shirt pocket and handed the little boy a candy bar. "Here, hide this in your book until lunch. You can have it for dessert!" Then he turned and slowly headed up the stairs to his classroom on the third floor. The little boy slipped the candy inside the front cover of his book and smiled all the way to his room.

For the rest of that school year, the little boy spent every recess at the baseball diamond. He was the only first-grader ever allowed to play there and often his was the only white face visible in a sea of brown. His parents began to notice some interesting (and amusing) slang in his language but they didn't say much about it. Sometimes the bigger boys let him play in the outfield and sometimes he just hung out behind the backstop with his new best friend, Marvin. He loved going to school again and he loved reading about Dick and Jane and their dog, Spot. And almost every day he had a Hershey Bar for lunch.

The Eternal Gift

If it is true we are all one in the Spirit or, in the language of quantum physics, that every element in the universe is a vital and interdependent part of a vast cosmic Unity, then no act of loving-kindness, no matter how small, is ever lost. It reverberates throughout the universe, touching everything and everyone, like the ripples on a pond when a tiny stone is dropped into the middle. The energy of Love is eternal.

The little boy in this story could easily have been conditioned by his experiences with the tall girl with the missing front tooth to believe all Black people are cruel and ugly and they always hate White people. This conviction-born-of-pain and the natural fear it would engender could have planted the seeds of racism deep within his heart. But when the Hershey Man picked up that book and handed it back with a kind word, he became the Christ to that little boy, an agent of forgiveness and reconciliation. And he quite possibly affected the course of that child's life and the gradual development of his compassion towards others who are different or in pain. As the proverb says, "When a butterfly flaps its wings in Tokyo, it rains in New York."

Let us resolve to flood the universe with our acts of loving-kindness. Let them ring forth from our hearts like the bells on Christmas Day. In our words and deeds, in our thoughts, and in our meditation, let us practice love and forgiveness in the firm belief that our actions, no matter how small or seemingly insignificant, will surely help to transform the world.

Epilogue

The following year, my father was transferred again, and I began the second grade in a new school in a different city. Even though I made many new friends, I never forgot about Marvin's kindness and his gentle ways. Even after thirty-five years, the Hershey Man remains one of my fondest memories of Christ's advent into my life.

MEDITATION: *Loving-Kindness*

Find a comfortable position to sit for a few minutes. Just relax into your body, being mindful of the feeling of your arms and legs. Allow your breath to come and go of itself. Let go of distracting thoughts and focus your attention on the present moment. Sit this way for a few minutes until you feel very relaxed and your mind is quiet.

In truth, we cannot love others unreservedly until we first learn to love and accept ourselves. So this meditation always begins with us. Reflect on yourself for a moment. Think about your strengths and weaknesses, your abilities and disabilities, and your successes and failures. Try to do so without judgment. Just be aware of the qualities of your life and personality without grasping or aversion. Gently open your heart to yourself and envelop your entire being in light and love. Now repeat the following words slowly to yourself with as much attention and openness as possible:

May I be well, happy, and peaceful. May no harm come to me. May no difficulties come to me. May no problems come to me. May I have the patience, courage, and understanding to meet and overcome whatever difficulties, problems, and failures in life that I do encounter. I love you.

Now, direct this love towards someone for whom you feel great love and affection. It could be a spouse, a friend, or a teacher—someone you like very much. Visualize them in your mind and say the following words as if that person were sitting right in front of you listening. Know that the love you direct to them in this moment will be received and will make a difference in their life.

May _____ be well, happy, and peaceful. May no harm come to you. May no difficulties come to you. May no problems come to you. May you have the patience, courage, and understanding to meet and overcome whatever difficulties, problems, and failures in life that you do encounter. I love you.

Picture another being for whom you feel great love and affection and repeat the meditation with their name at the beginning. Send forth your loving-kindness to this person with focused attention and an open heart. Embrace them with your love and know that they will receive it.

Repeat the meditation again, substituting the name of someone with whom you have been angry—someone whom you perceive has caused you harm in some way. Reflect on the truth that no one suffers from our anger as much as ourselves. See if you can let the anger go in this moment and see this person as a child of God. See them as your brother or your sister. See them as your own self. Say the words to them now—honestly, lovingly, and with complete forgiveness.

Finally, let your love expand to include your family, your neighborhood, your country, the entire world. Feel the spaciousness of that love. Sit with it. Be aware of the gentle stirrings in your heart and the lightness of your being. Let your loving-kindness expand until it embraces the entire universe. Notice the growing desire of your heart that all beings should share in this joy; no one should be excluded from this feast of love. Finish your time of meditation with these words:

May all living beings be well, happy, and peaceful. May no harm come to them. May no difficulties come to them. May no problems come to them. May they have the patience, courage, and understanding to meet and overcome whatever difficulties, problems, and failures in life that they do encounter. Amen.

■

12

FACING DEATH

All the greatest spiritual traditions of the world, including of course Christianity, have told us clearly that death is not the end. They have all handed down a vision of some sort of life to come, which infuses this life that we are leading now with sacred meaning. But despite their teachings modern society is largely a spiritual desert where the majority imagine that this life is all that there is. Without any real or authentic faith in an afterlife, most people live lives deprived of any ultimate meaning.

SOGYAL RINPOCHE

Meditations on death are a means of purifying the mind in order to gain a crucial revelation of the meaning and significance of life and death. As such, death meditations have been regarded as an indispensable element in a wide array of cultures: the Egyptian and Indian, the Chinese and Japanese, the Hellenic and Roman, the Hebrew and Islamic, in both their ancient and modern forms. Because of death's general unfathomableness and the dread and terror it inspires in most people, the conquest of death, or deathlessness, has a central place in the teachings of all religions. Unless this fear and terror is replaced by comfort and hope, a tranquil mind state is impossible. The unwillingness to think of death is itself a kind of death, for the poignancy of life is inseparable from the knowledge of its inevitable decay.

PHILIP KAPLEAU

I CAN'T imagine graduate study in any academic field is too much fun. Working on a doctoral degree in psychology when you have a wife and two small sons, a full-time college teaching position, and a growing private practice is certainly not something I would recommend. It's like having a third job you get to do in your spare time. Like late at night and on weekends.

I suppose graduate work is like any other job. Sometimes it is enjoyable, occasionally it can even be exciting, but usually it's tedious and exhausting. Why do it? That's a difficult question for a sane person to answer, assuming I am still sane after eight years of doctoral work. My honest answer is, "I don't know." Perhaps it was the result of some developmental abnormality in my early childhood or a misguided sense of divine purpose during my eighth-grade career day. Who knows? Maybe I did a doctorate for the same reason that motivates most forms of self-striving—to purchase the right to live.

In any doctoral program there are certain classes that everyone takes regardless of their area of specialization. At the university I attended these were called "core courses." The purpose of these courses, according to the catalogue, is to provide every psychology student with a broad exposure to the social sciences. Of course, most psychology students do not want a broad exposure to the social sciences, so what most core courses really offer is time to catch up on other reading.

There were some notable exceptions to this rule, including courses with such progressive and profound thinkers as Max Lerner, Anwar Dil, and Viktor Frankl. In their unique ways, each of these men knew how to reach out and embrace life. As Dr. Lerner once stated in class, "Plato once said that the unexamined life is not worth living. I would add that the unlived life is not worth examining!" For the most part, though, core courses were a test of academic endurance.

One particularly remarkable test of endurance was a course I took towards the end of my degree program entitled, "Futures: International Perspectives." It was taught by a stand-in professor who had been assigned to the course at the last minute due to the illness of the regular professor. He called himself a New Age Futurist and since I had no idea what a futurist was, I decided to listen for a while. What I heard for the entire quarter concerned his membership in something he called the "140 Club." From what I could gather, this is a group of earnest and sincere men and women who believe they will live to be 140 years old. Their basic philosophy is that people die because of wrong living and wrong thinking. We die because we are spiritually immature. We die because we think we're going to die; and if we will only change this faulty attitude, there will be no limit to how long we might live. And all this time I thought we die because we are mortal!

The Birth of New Age Guilt

As laughable as we all found this whole idea to be at the time, I have since come to see some merit in it. I do believe positive attitudes and right living can "increase the length of our days," within limits. So I eat red meat only about twice a month, I walk two miles every morning, and I try to love my neighbor as myself. What I do not believe is that I can somehow cheat death by my careful attention to right living and thinking. Herein lies the seeds of tremendous "New Age Guilt." If right living and thinking is the key to physical health and longevity, then it follows that if I become seriously or chronically ill then I must not be very enlightened. Larry Dossey, the author of several excellent books on spirituality and healing, is quoted as saying,

> *The other thing that I question is the new-age equation between spiritual achievement and physical health; that if I can just get wise enough, I will have perfect health. That's the new-age anthem.*
>
> *The slightest look at history denies that possibility. Many, or even most, of the wisest, most spiritually advanced people in history have died of some horrible disease: Krishnamurti, pancreatic cancer; Suzuki Roshi, gallbladder cancer; Ramana Maharshi, the most beloved saint in modern India, cancer of*

the stomach. Go further back in history: Saint Bernadette died of disseminated tuberculosis at the ripe age of thirty-three. The Buddha died of food poisoning. Tremendous levels of spiritual realization are no guarantee of a nice life with perfect health. Yet people continue to believe that if they just fix themselves up, just have enough positive thoughts and spiritual achievement, then they will have a really nice life. It just doesn't work out that way.[1]

The implication of this New-Age formula is that if I should die "before my time," I must be a spiritual pygmy. Dossey goes on to say,

Unless people understand this, the stage is set for an epidemic of new-age guilt. People who are on the spiritual path will have biopsies come back positive. Then they'll begin to beat up on themselves, engage in self-blame, feelings of guilt. They'll say, "If I had just been spiritual enough, the biopsy would have come back negative."[2]

The truth is, I am Infinite Mind manifesting Itself in a finite body, and this means I must one day cease to exist in my present physical state. This remains true no matter how I live, what I think, where I go, or how tenaciously I try to avoid the whole issue.

It seems most of us are pretty adept at doing just that—avoiding the whole issue. We don't consciously think about our own mortality except at those moments when we confront it directly, such as when a loved one dies or we experience a "near-miss" on the freeway. Most of the time we actively engage in denial without ever knowing we are doing it. We keep busy, we absorb ourselves in the day-to-day problems of work or family life, we struggle up the socio-economic ladder, we go to graduate school, or we join the 140 Club. There are as many ways to deny death as there are people in the world. But no matter how hard we try, we must ultimately deal with the reality of our own finitude.

The quality of our lives and the meaning and purpose of our existence can never really improve until we face the inevitability of our own mortality and eventually surrender it to God. This is not a new idea nor will it ever have much popular appeal. It threatens to expose us to our greatest fears. But it is forceful and potentially revolutionary in the lives of those who are able to summon the quaking courage to face it.

I was talking recently with a good friend of mine concerning this whole issue of facing our own mortality head-on in order to discover how to live more authentically. He decided to begin his own death meditations and as a result, he wrote his own eulogy. I found it so entertaining and inspiring I published it in the journal I edit for our "New Age Futurists" group (only kidding, it's really a spiritual study group). I have included it here in its entirety.[3]

A Simple Eulogy

The following should be read to those gathered after I have died. Now to be completely accurate, these pages should be blank. But, as always, I have chosen not to be completely accurate. Further in-sights may be gained by purchasing one of my books in the lobby.

Ever since my father died when I was nine I have been afraid of dying. At least I thought it was death that terrified me. But eventually I realized that what I feared was the total meaninglessness of life. If presidents and builders of pyramids, great artists and even my father could die without the world grinding to a halt, then what was the point? What could I possibly do that would make a difference, that would save me from everlasting extinction?

Some of you will know this feeling. Others of you, and I know who you are, will just smile and wonder why anyone would give it a second thought. Well, I have thought about it, often, and as a result have manifested what I'm sure to some seemed quite bizarre behavior. In fact, my seemingly unusual view of the world and whatever creative impulses I have ever had can be attributed to two things.

One is the view, more frequently held unconsciously than consciously, that life has absolutely no meaning, except of course, what we make up.

Secondly, and perhaps as a result of the first, I was never able to draw a distinction between what I could imagine and therefore what must be possible.

By the same token, I have been hindered by the same phenomenon because if I could not imagine it to its completion, I simply stood dazed like an animal caught in headlights and waited for more information. Oh well.

So now I'm dead and you're not. Or at least that's the way it appears. And if anyone is so inclined, please build a grave-bookstore-coffee bar complex for my remains so that people can come and visit. Not for my sake, but for theirs. It's good to carry on conversations with the dead because then all the questions and answers can only come from one place, which is what they do anyway. Only now someone else's chatter doesn't allow you to pretend that what you heard came from anyone but you.

By the way, I have recently discovered this about the meaning of life:

> **This horse walks into a bar and sits down to order a drink. The bartender walks over and says, "Hey, hey . . . why the long face?"**

Now, regarding my final words. There is a fascination with "dying words" and rightly so. We live only by and through language. In fact, I have read several books on the dying words of the famous and the infamous. My favorite one is, "My dying words are in the folder on the desk."

In my case, no matter what else you've heard, here are my dying words, the last thing I ever said, my departing logos: "Good night everybody. You've been a wonderful audience."

Facing Our Fear of Death

Directly confronting the inescapable reality of our own death accomplishes several important things in our lives. As we have discussed before, the conscious realization of death or nonbeing is one of our most primal and disruptive fears. Most of us run from this realization just as fast and as far as we can. It is the desperate need to deny this fear and the feeling of separation and alienation it engenders that empowers our self-defeating ego projects. And we know all too well where ego projects will take us sooner or later. They always fail and they always make a mess of things when they do. If all of this is true, then meditating on the mysterious cycles of life, death, and rebirth or transformation may free us to become more creative and less fear-motivated.

If I can learn to think about my own death with a certain amount of grace and peaceful acceptance, what is left for me to fear in this life? If I am able to defeat this greatest of all human terrors, all other fears will simply dissolve into hearty laughter. I mean, so what if the rent check is a week late because I broke my leg and haven't worked in a month? What are you going to do, kill me? I don't think so. Besides, as Jesus once said, "Don't be afraid of those who can kill your body. Rather, fear those who can destroy your soul."[4] Since no one could possibly do that, I have nothing to fear.

If I am not always worried about this possible complication or that negative eventuality, what becomes of my desperate need to engineer and maintain an ego project that virtually guarantees a life of unremitting anxiety and mental agitation? When the mind is no longer fearful and noisy, constantly jumping from one thought or concern to the next, what happens to the ego? And what happens to my unquestioning identification with this weak and mortal self I think I am?

Under such conditions, I will begin to slowly detach from my tiny conception of self as it is defined by the ego and the physical body and start to identify with a far greater Reality. I may even begin to experience my Oneness with all Being which is our true inheritance. As Krishnamurti was fond of saying, we are really the owners of a vast estate who have become content with living in a tiny little corner of the field. And in living there for so long, we have come to believe our tiny little corner is all there is. Somehow we must open our eyes to the truth of our position in eternity. We are One. This life of separateness and pain is nothing more than an illusion, a mere shadow of our true existence.

Meditating on death and surrendering our fearfulness is one way to begin restoring our sight so we can live freely in the land of Love. As Marcus Aurelius (A.D. 121–180), the Roman emperor and Stoic philosopher, once wrote, "The constant recollection of death is the test of human conduct."[5] It is also a reliable path to human transformation.

As I become more identified with my real Self and less enamored with the world of apparent physical realities, a positive synergy begins to operate in my life. I will experience my own eternalness directly, without intellection and without doubt. I will no longer need to engage in theological discussion or intellectual debate as to whether or not the human soul is eternal. I will simply know I AM. And this knowledge will reduce my fear of death even further for I will realize that death is not the end of being but only a transition from one learning experience to the next. It may even enable me to begin trusting Life instead of feeling like I must always be in control. This is surely the "peace that passes all understanding."

One final note. When I no longer fear my own physical demise, I will probably stop working so hard at meaningless tasks that take me away from more important pursuits. Instead of going to a meeting of the "140 Club" or working sixty hours a week to try and purchase some measure of immortality through my project, maybe I'll just take my boys to a Dodger game.

MEDITATION: *On Death and Dying*

There are only two choices while we are here.
We can choose a living death or
we can lead a dying life.

Begin this meditation by writing your own eulogy. It doesn't have to be long or involved, it just needs to state those things for which you would like to be remembered. Make it serious or humorous, whatever you like, but make sure it is an open and honest description of your hopes and dreams and your strengths and weaknesses. Talk about the experiences that taught you the most about life and truth. Talk about the people you love, and what they mean to you. Then tell them each goodbye. End your eulogy with the phrase or statement you would like to have carved on your headstone. Finally, tape record the entire thing so you can play it back during the second part of this meditation.

Sit down in a comfortable position, with your back straight and your mind alert. Have the tape recorder next to you, ready to play the eulogy. Let your eyes rest easily on this page, and focus on the natural in-and-out rhythm of your breathing. Envision your breath to be like the cycles of the ocean tides in miniature. The breath flows in, the breath flows out. Over and over again. Follow the sensations closely, wherever you feel them the most. Let your body melt into the chair or the cushion.

Imagine that each time you inhale, you are breathing in peacefulness and healing and Grace. And each time you exhale, imagine you are breathing away fear and tension and anxiety. In this way, each cycle of your breath purifies your awareness and strengthens your attention. Continue to focus on your breathing for the next several minutes.

Now, imagine yourself at your own funeral, even as you

continue to focus on the rhythm of your breathing. There, in the front of the church, synagogue, or funeral home, is your casket (or urn) which contains all that's left of your earthly body. The front pew is filled with your spouse and children and grandchildren. You see the tears in their eyes as they remember your life and mourn your loss. (*Stay with your breath.*) The room is filled with your friends and other family members, whispering quietly to one another in hushed tones as they reminisce about your life. You are genuinely surprised and pleased by how many people have chosen to attend your memorial.

(*Now reach over and hit the play button on the tape recorder.*) Listen to your own words and try to imagine how your friends and family are feeling right now. Be aware of their sadness and of their love for you. Send them loving-kindness wordlessly, as you continue to be aware of the sensations of your breath. Comfort them with your love and reassure them of your well-being. Listen to the tape as you say your last goodbyes, and feel the strange mixture of sorrow and peace in your own heart.

When the eulogy is finished, turn off the tape and return to meditating on your breath. Let each breath go out unhindered, as if it were your last. Don't hold on to it. Don't hold on to anything, not even to life. We must learn to travel light. Surrender yourself completely with each outgoing breath—gently, easily, painlessly. Let go into the Light.

■

13

IN REMEMBRANCE

For I am convinced that neither death, nor life, nor angels, nor principalities, nor things present, nor things to come, nor powers, nor height, nor depth, nor any other created thing, shall be able to separate us from the love of God, which is in Christ Jesus our Lord.

ST. PAUL

How do I know that loving life is not a delusion? How do I know that in hating death I am not like a man who, having left home in his youth, has forgotten the way back?

CHUANG TZU

I FIRST met Sandra in 1988. She was referred to me by her neighbor whom I had seen for marital therapy the previous year. She arrived for our first session dressed in tight-fitting jeans, a baggy T-shirt, and loose sandals which she kicked off as soon as she sat down. As I would learn in the months ahead, this was Sandra's standard "uniform." I would also learn she hated wearing shoes and would take them off whenever she was going to be in the same room for more than two minutes.

She was only about 5'5" in height, but she seemed much taller because she was so extremely thin. She had short, dishwater blond hair that curled haphazardly around her angular face. She also had the clearest ice-blue eyes I had ever seen. They were the color of sky and water, the water of a high mountain lake. It was her eyes that always caught your attention first. You could see fire in those eyes. Fire and ice.

As we began talking in that first session, Sandra's speech was rapid and pressured, her thoughts were often tangential and confused, and she could hardly sit still. She had small sores or "speed bumps" on her neck and arms. It was obvious she was under the influence of amphetamines. When I commented on my observations, Sandra became extremely agitated and defensive. After a few tense moments, during which I wondered if I had moved too quickly, she began telling her story:

She had been using "speed" and other illegal drugs almost daily since the age of twelve. The only time she had stopped was when she was pregnant with her son, now three years old. She made it very clear she didn't want any help with her drug problem even though she admitted to being a gram-a-day user. She told me she had left her last therapist after only two sessions because he had recommended immediate hospitalization in order to help her "get clean." This was her way of telling me in no uncertain terms I had better not make the same stupid mistake.

Sandra spent the remainder of that initial session telling me in great detail about the many problems she was having with her second husband. She had married the first time at nineteen and had remained married for about five years. She finally got a divorce because her husband had beaten her frequently and had often threatened to kill her. Her second husband, whom she met and married shortly thereafter, was not physically abusive; but she found him to be overly dependent on her for emotional support and very irresponsible with money. It was quite evident these were the only issues that Sandra was willing to discuss. So I listened to her disjointed monologue and did not press the subject of her drug dependence any further that evening. When our time was over, she agreed to see me again in a few days. As she left my office to schedule her next appointment at the front desk, I remember thinking I would probably never see her again.

In the days following that first session, I reflected on the fact that Sandra was one of the most angry and frightened people I had ever met. I knew from training and experience that her hardened exterior probably concealed deep-seated insecurities and a tremendous feeling of vulnerability. I was certain her aggressiveness towards anything or anyone that seemed to threaten her fragile world was really a heart-rending request for love. I also realized I would never be able to help her put her life back together until she was willing to confront and deal with her addiction.

I couldn't help but wonder what kind of childhood experiences could have driven Sandra into the world of drugs at such an early age. Was it trauma of some kind, such as physical or sexual abuse, peer pressure she had no power to resist, or simply adolescent rebellion that remained unchecked by appropriate parental limits? Any or all of these situations could explain her behavior and subsequent lifestyle, but at that point I had very few clues. It would probably take a long time for Sandra to establish sufficient trust to allow me to uncover the answers to these questions. Provided, of course, she showed up for her next session.

When Sandra arrived for her second session, I was both pleased and a little surprised. Apparently I had passed the first test, but I took no comfort in that fact. I had decided the night before I was going to talk to her about hospitalization for her extreme drug dependency. I was sure I was about to flunk the second test in a big way, but I didn't feel I had any other choice. The drugs were going to kill her. Maybe not today or tomorrow, but someday.

She came into my office once again dressed in blue jeans and a baggy shirt, plopped down on the sofa, kicked off her cowboy boots, and folded her legs underneath her. She looked extremely lethargic and depressed. Gone was the manic energy and verbal onslaught of our previous session. When she spoke, she stuttered and her voice quivered and she carefully avoided eye contact with me. She responded to my questions and comments with one- or two-word answers and then fell silent for minutes at a time. When I asked why she was feeling so down, she said she had been unable to afford any drugs for the past two days and was in the middle of "sketching," or coming down.

Over the years, I have seen hundreds of cases of serious depression in both inpatient and outpatient settings. I knew Sandra's depression was severe and potentially dangerous. I spent the remainder of the session talking to her about the pros and cons of hospitalization for both her chemical dependency and depression. Although she resisted the idea at first, her opposition was only token. I think she was just too tired to fight back at that moment. I called the hospital and arranged to have her admitted that same night.

The Eye of the Storm

So began a two-year odyssey of pain and hope, minor victories and serious setbacks. During that two-year period, Sandra was hospitalized on eight separate occasions (not counting overnight stays in county emergency rooms), often for as long as three months. She was also admitted to three different drug rehabilitation "halfway houses," but she never stayed in these for more than a day or two before she went AWOL. She always told me these places had too many rules. Sandra hated rules and usually went out of her way to break them.

It was during her first hospitalization that Sandra began to remember previously repressed memories of childhood molestation. Through the use of clinical hypnosis and other uncovering techniques, we discovered that her abuse began at about the age of five or six and continued into her teenage years. She was raped by several people over the years including various friends of her older brother, her mother's live-in boyfriend, and the brother of one of her baby-sitters. Without going into further detail, suffice it to say the nature of the abuse she was made to endure was perverse and chronic. The intense shame and anger caused by this abuse was what led Sandra into the world of drugs. At the tender age of twelve, she was already trying to medicate away her pain.

As memories of the abuse continued to emerge in therapy, Sandra became increasingly angry, belligerent, and self-destructive. She began cutting herself with razor blades until her legs and arms were covered with scars. She would put her fist through walls or tear up her hospital room whenever she didn't like what a nurse or doctor said or did, which was often. I intervened with the nursing staff on numerous occasions to keep her from being transferred to the intensive therapy unit (ITU) after her latest episode of acting-out behavior.

In most psychiatric hospitals, intensive therapy unit is an oxymoron. It is a locked unit, usually in the oldest part of the hospital, where therapy is rarely attempted, let alone accomplished. The only thing that is intensive is the smell of feces and urine.

Sometimes I could diffuse the situation enough so the admitting psychiatrist would allow Sandra to remain on the open unit. At other times, I could not. I remember being called at home late one night because she had climbed the scaffolding to the top of the new three-story hospital wing that was still under construction. When I arrived at the hospital, she was dancing on the girders with a bottle of contraband tequila in her hand. It took me almost a week to get her released from the ITU on that occasion.

Sandra's behavior during this period was always provocative. It was designed to create chaos and outrage among those people who cared about her. I think it was simply an outward expression of the chaos and outrage she felt inside her own mind. But there was one thing I was always sure of with Sandra. She would never inflict physical pain on others. She could yell and scream and cuss better than a drunken sailor. But she would never cause you serious harm, unless you think of a bruised ego as serious. Buried deep beneath her overwhelming pain was a tender heart that longed to reach out to other people. It was the fear that stopped her.

Every time Sandra left the hospital she went back to the drugs within a few days. Even though I would see her in therapy three or four times each week, I was unable to stop the freight train of her self-destructive behavior. Sometime during her second year in treatment, she began to experiment with suicidal gestures and attempts. These would usually consist of taking an overdose of her antidepressant medication or slicing her arm or leg near an artery. Then she would call me in the middle of the night to tell me what she had done. I soon lost count of the number of times I called the paramedics and then stood in the emergency room watching her have her stomach pumped or her arm stitched.

At some level, I knew that these suicidal "dramas" were Sandra's way of testing my resolve. She was still trying to figure out if I could be trusted. The reality she had grown up with as a child was that everyone would betray her sooner or later and that love always results in abandonment and pain. I think she honestly wanted to believe my statements of caring and commitment were real. But there was another part of her that wanted to prove I was a liar like all the rest.

In addition to her testing of my commitment, I was aware of a more dangerous and insidious process occurring as well. Sandra was slowly beginning to desensitize herself to the fear of committing suicide. With each successive gesture, she would take two or three more pills or cut herself just a little deeper. Not only was she challenging my resolve, she was pushing the boundaries of her own. I knew I somehow had to prove to Sandra that trust is not always betrayed, love does not always end in pain, and forgiveness will always bring healing.

Fire and Ice

I must have failed to convince her of these things. As I write this, Sandra has been gone for a little more than two months. She died on a Sunday afternoon in the home of a friend after injecting herself with a lethal dose of speed. Shortly after the paramedics failed to revive her, the friend called me at home.

Hearing the details of Sandra's last day on earth and of her death, I felt a tremendous heaviness invade my heart. When I hung up the phone, I could think of nothing else to do but go out on the patio and pray under the trees while the tears coursed down my face.

The next few days were spent dealing with various friends and members of Sandra's family, seeing my normal case load of patients, and trying to cope with my own pain and grief. I must have asked myself a hundred times how I could have done things differently with Sandra. How had I failed her? Should I have been more confrontive about her self-destructive behaviors or was I too confrontive? Maybe I didn't take her feelings seriously enough. Should I have been more supportive, or was I too supportive—thereby acting as an enabler? I bombarded myself with endless questions and the answers always seemed to elude me. After several days of painful and confusing introspection, I realized these questions would have to be addressed at another time. What I needed to do right then was to grieve the loss of someone I cared about deeply. I needed to find a way to say goodbye to Sandra.

When Sandra's mother asked me to speak at the memorial service, I wanted very much to decline. I didn't think there was anything I could possibly say that could give meaning to this tragedy. I had not yet been able to find any meaning in it for myself, so how could I possibly speak to others of her life? After much internal struggle, I finally agreed to participate.

I purposely did not write any notes or prepare any formal comments. There was never anything formal or stuffy about Sandra, and I didn't think she would appreciate a flowery eulogy. Besides, I wanted to be able to speak spontaneously from my heart. What follows are the closing words of my goodbye to Sandra, as well as I can recall them.

"There is no life that is lived in vain. Every life is a story that has the power to bless those who hear it or watch it unfold. The blessing Sandra's life bestows upon us is this: we must allow

ourselves to be loved. If we insist on holding ourselves separate from one another because of fear or pain or disappointment, we will all die inside. It is by freely giving and receiving love we are able to catch a glimpse of our essential oneness. Only love can teach us the greatest truth: we are all children of the same Father.

Sandra, I know you were just too scared to let me or anyone else really love you. You kept us all at arm's length while you charmed us with your blue jeans and cowboy boots and infuriated us with your adolescent stubbornness. But I saw it . . . more than once. Oh, you know I did! That tender place in your heart you protected with all the power of a lioness. It bugged you to no end that I could see it.

You wanted to pretend your heart was cold and tough and you didn't care about anyone. But I knew better . . . and so did you. You even as much as admitted it to me once while we were sitting in the emergency room of Circle City Hospital, waiting to get your arm stitched up again. As you applied pressure to your arm, you talked about your son and how much you loved him. Tears leaked traitorously from your eyes. You tried to recover by making some kind of a joke but it was too late. I'd already seen your hidden garden and you knew it. The brief smile you flashed at me said it was okay that I knew.

I wish you would have let us in more often, Sandra. Maybe we could have shown you that love doesn't always have to hurt. I know you have finally found the peace you always longed for. I wish to God you could have found that peace here, with us. I will miss you, Sandra. We will all miss you. Kyrie Eleison. God have mercy."

14

RESURRECTION

For now we see in a mirror dimly, but then face to face; now I know in part, but then I shall know fully just as I also have been fully known.

St. Paul

Very simply, the resurrection is the overcoming or surmounting of death. It is a reawakening or a rebirth; a change of mind about the meaning of the world. All living hearts are tranquil with a stir of deep anticipation, for the time of everlasting things is now at hand. There is no death. The Son of God is free. And in his freedom is the end of fear.

A Course in Miracles

AS I WRITE this chapter, I am camping with my family in an outdoor cathedral. It is a classroom where semi-somnambulant city dwellers can relearn their childhood skills of awe and wonder. It is a place where the human spirit can no longer restrain itself from reaching out to touch the loving face of God. You may know it as the Yosemite Valley, but it is really the ancient geography of our collective soul. Everyone who comes here is invited to commune with the divine nature within them and be transformed by its quiet and persuasive power.

I am sitting at the picnic table in our campsite (North Pines, #78), listening to music on our portable compact disc/AM-FM radio/cassette recorder (I said we are camping but I didn't say anything about roughing it). A few moments ago, Eric Clapton began to sing "Tears in Heaven," just as I looked up at the marvelous granite face of Half Dome. As I contemplate this glacial wonder, I am listening closely to the words of this bittersweet tribute to his four-year-old son who died tragically a couple of years ago. Tears are welling up in my eyes and I can hardly see Half Dome.

To tell you the truth, I'm not sure why I am crying. Maybe it is just the combination of beautiful scenery and melancholy music. Maybe it puts me in mind of my own son and Cystic Fibrosis. But I suspect my tears are also for a little boy who took a terrible fall out of a high-rise apartment building and can no longer bring sunshine into his parents' lives. I cry, too, for a father with the courage to write a song for his lost child and then perform it in front of thousands of people. As I wipe the tears from my eyes, I think about the mysterious blessing hidden within this tragedy.

The Prison of Perception

It didn't take me long after becoming a therapist to realize people perceive the world differently—sometimes very differently. Not only do we each form different perceptions or images of our world, ourselves, and each other; but we devote vast amounts of time and energy rationalizing, defending, and promoting the rightness or truth of our images. Sounds crazy doesn't it?

Take a typical example. Let's say I "image" myself as a very loving and generous person who genuinely enjoys helping others with their problems. You casually mention your garage is pretty messy, so I kindly offer to help you clean it. I see my behavior as being consistent with the images I hold of myself and my world. But what would happen if you, on the other hand, held a very different image of me? What if you saw me as a basically compulsive and controlling person who likes nothing more than to meddle in other people's business? I suspect this image would radically alter your perception of my intentions for offering to help you. You might even refuse my offer, which would only serve to reinforce my image of you as an ungrateful troll who would rather clean his garage by himself than owe someone a favor! On the other hand, you might decide to accept my offer because the garage is really bad but then resent every attempt on my part to help you get organized. All because you see my actions as controlling and therefore disrespectful of your abilities.

Here lies fertile ground for misunderstanding, anger, and even hatred. All because you can't keep your garage clean! No, actually it is because you and I can't agree about the images and perceptions we are constantly projecting onto the world and each other. People and nations go to war for no other reason than to assert the superiority of their images.

In this example, who is right and who is wrong? Am I a generous and loving person or am I compulsive and controlling? The truth is I am both and neither of these things depending upon when you look at me. I change too quickly for any perception based on past experience to be accurate. Everyone does. Images, judgments, and perceptions are not real or true or accurate or even very helpful because they are always, by definition, outdated. Reality just moves too fast to be accurately contained in an image. Our perceptions almost guarantee we will not be able to see the truth about one another or the world around us. Since this is the case, we might at least spend some time trying to understand the nature and origin of these images that control our lives.

First of all, where do these images come from? How are they formed? Perceptions develop slowly over the course of our lives through the cumulative judgments of our intellect and our emotions or feeling states. The raw material for these judgments is supplied by such things as the structure and function of our sensory apparatus (we can only see what our eyes are structured to see), our temperament and personality characteristics, our religious and cultural heritage, socio-economic status, and family background as well as our total life-experiences. In other words, our perceptions of the world are shaped by a number of processes nobody but a demented social scientist would care to think about.

All of these processes serve as perceptual filters through which we come to see and understand ourselves and our world. Because there are so many of these variables that combine in unique patterns for each individual, there is a tremendous degree of diversity in what people call reality. In fact, no two people could possibly see the world in exactly the same way from the egoic level of understanding. There is just too much room for diversity.

So here I sit with my idiosyncratic collection of images and beliefs, both consciously and unconsciously created by the complex interaction of literally hundreds of perceptual processes, most of which are unique to my experience and genetic inheritance. This "perceptual stew" is what I come to call the truth (actually, it would be more accurate to call it the ego). It never even occurs to me that the world I "see" and take for granted is already several levels removed from the truth—that it is only a dim reflection of Pure Reality (Yes Virginia, Plato and St. Paul were right).

Now, if my images of life happen to be somewhat consistent with yours and if our perceptions of one another when we meet are fairly similar to each of our own self-perceptions, we might be able to become friends and sustain a "relationship." Though it seems to me that two sets of inherently distorted images bumping into each other for a few minutes or a few years can hardly be called a relationship.

What would happen if one of us made a radical change in our fundamental perception of life (like becoming a Democrat)? What would become of our relationship? No matter what we might want to believe about love and mutual tolerance and nonjudgmental acceptance, if the change in my behavior, beliefs, or perceptions is enough to threaten the security of your system of images, and if I am unable to persuade you to change your views or at least tolerate mine, our relationship will most certainly change and may even come to an end. In life as it is usually lived, perceptual images are more important to preserve than relationships.

The real problem with all of this is we never really "see" one another or ourselves as we truly are. Our vision is constantly being filtered by preconceived notions based on past experiences and conditioning. Neither of us is able to see life or one another freely and spontaneously.

Imagine what it would be like if we were all born with perfect eyesight but at birth someone attached a pair of glasses to our faces that distorted our vision. We would soon adjust to the distortion and what we saw through our glasses would become our "reality." Now imagine that each year of our lives, the lenses became thicker and more distorted and we gradually forgot we were even wearing glasses.

This is exactly what images do to us. Our relationships (especially our relationship to God) are constantly being distorted by perceptions and judgments formed around outdated historical information (it is outdated if it is more than two seconds old). This information has very little, if anything, to do with who we really are at the moment.

This may be the reason why God told us to make no graven images and to have no other "gods" before Him. He wasn't just talking about golden calves. He was talking about limited human perceptions that separate us from the Truth. We must learn how to remove our coke-bottle glasses, and as William Blake once wrote, "see reality as it truly is—eternal."

Our greatest Western mystic, Meister Eckhart, asserted we can never really know God face to face until we abandon all "images" we might have of him. His exact words were, "I pray God to rid me of God!"

Maybe the same is true on the human level. Maybe I can

never really know you until I am able to abandon all of my images of you. And until we "know" each other we cannot have a relationship; we can never really touch. J. Krishnamurti once wrote,

> *Seeing is to be intimately in contact with life and you cannot be intimately, actually in contact with it if you have concepts, beliefs, dogmas, or opinions. So what is important is not to learn but to see and to listen. Listen to the birds, listen to your wife's voice, however irritating, beautiful or ugly, listen to it and listen to your own voice however beautiful, ugly, or impatient it may be. Then out of this listening you will find that all separation between the observer and the observed comes to an end. Therefore no conflict exists and you observe so carefully that the very observation is discipline; you don't have to impose discipline. And that is the beauty Sirs (if only you realize it), that is the beauty of seeing. If you can see, you have nothing else to do, because in that seeing there is all discipline, all virtue, which is attention. And in that seeing there is all beauty, and with beauty there is love. Then when there is love you have nothing more to do. Then where you are, you have heaven; then all seeking comes to an end.*[1]

Did you hear that? All separation between the observer and the observed comes to an end! Is he serious? He is actually proposing that if we can figure out how to see life directly—without images, without preconceptions and deeply-held opinions, just see it—we will experience our essential oneness with all being. We will no longer just be talking and theorizing about the unity of life and the universality of love, we will be living it out of our own truest essence from moment to moment to eternity. And all we have to do is take our glasses off.

Can this be true? Can this be done? Is it possible for humans to be so "pure in heart" we could actually see and experience God in everyone and everything? And if it is possible, what's stopping us? These are questions we can no longer avoid putting to ourselves. We must answer them now, for ourselves alone. Heaven and hell, life and death, love and loneliness may well hang in the balance.

Having Eyes to See

I think Jesus was one who succeeded in answering these questions. His entire ministry is an example of what Zen calls "direct seeing" into the nature of reality. If we had been with Jesus when he met the Samaritan woman at the well, what would we have seen? A woman of an oppressed ethnic group? A prostitute? He saw an honest seeker of considerable spiritual sensitivity who was ready to take the next step of realization. That she learned to "see" that day demonstrates how Christ's vision was able to move her toward transformation. And what about the time when he fed the five thousand? We would have seen only a little boy with five loaves and two fish. He saw the unlimited supply of heaven itself spread before everyone.

We call these things miracles, but Jesus never referred to them as such. To someone who is no longer burdened by all of the ideas, dogmas, and perceptions that separate people from the knowledge of who they really are, the "miraculous" seems normal and natural. We might say in response to this, "Yes, but he is the Son of God." I suspect Christ or Buddha or Krishna would reply, "Well, who do you think you are? Bozo the clown?"

So what stops me from "seeing" reality, God, my neighbor? What is it that grips my heart with fear every time I consider abandoning my safe and secure concepts of life? Quite simply, to do so feels like dying. If I surrender my ego and become less "attached" to people and things—if I diligently practice forgiveness and love towards myself and my neighbor, transforming my vision of both—what becomes of the "me" I have come to know? Doesn't it experience a kind of death? And isn't death our greatest fear, our most powerful illusion?

In *The Denial of Death*, Ernest Becker wrote that we have a symbolic identity, a superior consciousness which brings us sharply out of nature and enables us to create almost anything we can imagine. But there is a high price to pay for a self-conscious and self-aware mind that enables us to soar to such imaginative heights. We are finite creatures who cannot escape a temporal and spatial body that is subject to illness and death. And because of our self-consciousness, we are the only creature that can contemplate this death. In Becker's prosaic words,

> *This is the paradox: he is out of nature and hopelessly in it; he is dual, up to the stars and yet housed in a heart-pumping, breath-gasping body that once belonged to a fish and still carries the gillmarks to prove it. His body is a material fleshy casing that is alien to him in many ways—the strangest and most repugnant way being that it aches and bleeds and will decay and die. Man is literally split in two: he has an awareness of his own splendid uniqueness in that he sticks out of nature with a towering majesty, and yet he goes back into the ground a few feet in order blindly and dumbly to rot and disappear forever.*[2]

As we have discussed, Becker and other existential philosophers believe this awareness of our own temporal finitude and the inevitable fear of death it produces is so powerful, so terrifying, and so ever-present that it serves to motivate all human endeavor in one guise or another. As a result, most people will religiously avoid any activity that feels to them like death or dying (unless they find a sense of power in activities that directly challenge death). Abandoning our images and surrendering to the unknown definitely qualifies as an activity that feels like dying!

The fear of death is an inevitable legacy of our ability to be self-conscious creatures and this fear (or the denial of it) motivates human behavior. Add the spiritual truth that fear is contrary to love and prevents us from being able to experience the peace and presence of God. We humans are caught in an incredible paradox. I cannot be free of my images and perceptions in order to experience Reality or abide in the presence of God as long as I am afraid. But to consider abandoning my very self in order to transcend to something completely unknown stimulates my greatest terror: the fear of death or nonbeing.

I am caught like a dying animal in a trap and the means of my escape is just beyond my reach. But what would become of this seemingly inescapable dilemma if something were to happen that convinced me, beyond the shadow of a doubt, that death is not real—nonbeing is an absolute impossibility? Would this not relieve my terror enough to allow me entry back into the Garden? And if it is true that death is our greatest illusion, what would happen to all of the "lesser" images and illusions I spend my life creating in order to distract myself from this ultimate fear? They would simply evaporate into stillness.

Well . . . something has happened that has the power to free us forever. For in the moment we truly understand and accept the promise of Easter, the promise of eternal life, in that very same moment we are reunited with the Source of all love and all life. Herein lies the secret blessing of the resurrection—death is not real! It is simply a hoax perpetrated upon us by our own egos.

Epilogue

The evening shadows are beginning to draw a silvery veil over the face of Half Dome. As I shiver in the fading light of this incredible day, I think of the Gospel, the Good News of the Christ and of all the Avatars throughout history. We are eternal beings, created by Love to abide forever within the arms of God. We have come to this far country for a brief moment to learn whatever it is we need to learn. Then we get to go Home. There is no such thing as death. There is only homecoming! Little boys who fall out of apartment windows do not die. Children with Cystic Fibrosis do not die. We do not die. We are already risen.

15

FORGIVENESS

Forgiveness means reconciliation in spite of estrangement; it means reunion in spite of hostility; it means acceptance of those who are unacceptable, and it means reception of those who are rejected.

PAUL TILLICH

All this beauty will rise to bless your sight as you look upon the world with forgiving eyes. For forgiveness literally transforms vision, and lets you see the real world reaching quietly and gently across chaos, removing all illusions that had twisted your perception and fixed it on the past. The smallest leaf becomes a thing of wonder, and a blade of grass a sign of God's perfection.

A COURSE IN MIRACLES

FORGIVENESS and grace are not easy skills to master. It is so much easier and more fun to be angry and to hold a grudge. Doesn't it feel *good* to be righteously indignant, to feel completely justified in your anger and then to walk away after having the last word? Well, this is certainly what the ego would have us believe.

The ego has declared itself to be a "self" that is separate from God and from all of creation. Like Esau, it has sold its birthright for a bowl of soup. It is therefore condemned to live in a state of constant fear and isolation until such time as it comes to its senses.

Because these are such vulnerable emotions, the ego covers them over with a layer of anger and frustration. It then encourages us to search around outside ourselves for people and situations we can blame for this anger. After all, if I'm this mad, I must have a good reason. So I look around until I find something in your life or in your behavior that angers or offends me and I judge you harshly for it.

Sooner or later, you will become aware of my judgment and begin to defend yourself or even retaliate with harsher judgments of your own. Of course, I will completely deny the fact that my judgments of you came first. This denial enables me to remain totally blind to the circular nature of our interactions. Therefore, I bear no responsibility for how you treat me. Your "unfair" reaction only serves to prove that my negative judgments of you were correct in the first place! And so it goes.

As a psychologist, I have become convinced through the years that unforgiveness is quite simply the "root of all evil" (or, if you prefer, karma) when it comes to human relationships. Every relational problem begins in the same way. There are always two angry, righteously indignant people who both feel they have been wronged and are both unwilling to let go of their anger and forgive. When we refuse to offer grace and forgiveness to one another, no matter what we may perceive the crime to be, we automatically exclude ourselves from the source of unconditional grace as well. In other words, my unforgiveness hurts no one as much as it hurts me. If I am unwilling to perceive the innocent face of Christ in you, how can I possibly recognize my own innocence? And if I cannot accept the atonement for myself, I will have to keep projecting my guilt onto you and encounter it there.

I am also convinced that unforgiveness serves as a veil between ourselves and the knowledge of our true identity. It paints the world with guilt and fear and blinds us to our essential Unity. The constant state of agitation it creates and maintains in our minds can only prolong the day of our awakening. We must learn to forgive now, both freely and without condition, if we would have our vision transformed and our lives filled with peace. Practicing forgiveness may well be our highest calling on the spiritual journey. Let me share a event in my life that taught me much about the transformational power of unconditional and undeserved grace.

The Wages of Sin and Karma

I don't know what it is about young boys and bodies of water but the two just seem to go together. Whether it is a puddle, a pond, a lake, or an ocean, there will always be plenty of boys on hand to kick, splash, wade, and wallow to ensure everyone within thirty feet receives a proper baptism. Maybe the negative ions that collect in the air above the water stimulate the production of testosterone. I just don't know.

In the town where I grew up in eastern Washington, there was a big pond across the street from the junior high school. It wasn't a pond really, more like a cesspool. It was tucked behind some houses and surrounded by trees and marsh grass, so it was easy to miss if you didn't know it was there. The thing that I remember most vividly was there were always a lot of fuzzy cattails growing along the edge of the water. The pond wasn't extremely large, perhaps only fifty yards wide and a hundred and fifty yards long, but it was huge by our youthful standards. It was supplied by the town's storm drains, so we are not talking pure mountain spring water here. But it had all the necessary ingredients boys find so irresistible: frogs for gigging, tadpoles for scooping into Mason jars, and homemade wooden rafts for paddling.

All my friends had been to the pond at one time or another and had wonderful stories to tell about their adventures. My parents had strictly forbidden me to go there, probably because they didn't think typhoid was a good idea for one so young. Based on my thirteen years of accumulated wisdom at that time, I was certain they were being unnecessarily overprotective and had quite probably entered into a secret conspiracy to prevent me from ever having any fun or adventure in my life. A conspiracy, I might add, that did not apply to the behavior of my two younger brothers!

Now my father, who had told me never to go near this pond, is a big man. He is about 5'10" tall and tips the scales at about 260 (sorry Dad, but this is a *nonfiction* book). His upper arms look like tree trunks and he can still bring me to my knees in a hand-squeezing contest (he cheats). You can imagine what an imposing figure he was to me as a boy.

My father also had a temper. When I was a child he could put the fear of God into me with just the snap of his fingers, a sound we kids dubbed "the snap from hell." One time, when I was whispering in church with my friends, we must have gotten a little too loud. All of a sudden, my father SNAPPED his big, meaty fingers from somewhere in the back of the sanctuary. I swear it sounded like a twelve-gauge shotgun going off. Talk about jumping to attention! I think dad even startled the pastor because he stopped preaching in mid-sentence and hurriedly reached for a drink of water. The poor man probably thought he had just preached down thunder from heaven. In my opinion, he was looking in exactly the wrong direction.

Nevertheless, one bright summer day the guys came to me and said they were going to the pond in search of adventure. Something about the Holy Grail or buried treasure, I think. I patiently explained I had been forbidden to go there by my parents and to disobey and be caught would be highly unpleasant (my dad had been known to favor a wide leather belt in matters of discipline with his sons). Things get a little fuzzy in my memory at this point. I am fairly certain that the word "chicken" came up at least once.

The next thing I knew, we were all walking the two miles to the pond—carrying our baseball equipment and talking excitedly about catching frogs. I think this must mean we told my mom we were going to the junior high to play ball. Of course there were several schoolyards with perfectly functional baseball diamonds that were much closer to my house than the junior high. This fact, I would learn later, was not completely lost on my mother. She could tell if I had been in the cupboards just by looking for my fingerprints on the chrome handles! When she suspected I had been smoking one time, she didn't smell my breath (which I had disguised with cinnamon Certs). She smelled the first two fingers of my right hand. I didn't even think of that.

During our entire journey to the pond, I firmly resolved I would just go there to get a good look at the place; and I would not, under any circumstances, get wet. After all, I was wearing blue jeans instead of cut-off shorts or a swimsuit like everyone else. Given my wardrobe selection for the day, I was sure my loyal compadres would understand my dilemma and go swimming and rafting without me while I just watched from the periphery of the shore. Right.

The pond was everything I dreamed it would be and more. There was a marvelous profusion of cattails swaying in the summer breeze that were perfect for swordfighting until the ends exploded into fluff. There were also at least three or four home-made rafts parked among the reeds and marsh grass, just waiting to be boarded by a band of baseball-playing pirates.

As soon as we got there, I walked to the edge of the water. There were literally thousands of tadpoles and tiny fish swimming within easy reach. As I bent over to get a better look, my friend, Mitch, kicked me so that I fell on my hands and knees in the water. So much for not getting wet.

Before long, we had split up into two-man rafting teams and were involved in a hormone-induced frenzy of laughing, splashing, paddling, racing, and dunking to see who would emerge victorious. To be honest, I don't even remember the object of the game—except I know it was intended to separate the men from the boys. It was also intended to get everyone soaked. On that count, it was extremely successful.

I remember I had just risen to my feet in full battle cry when, out of the corner of my eye, I caught a glimpse of my father's pea-green, 1960 Buick LeSabre turning slowly onto the dirt access road that ran along the length of the pond. It was hard to miss that car even in the heat of battle. Not only was the color reminiscent of bile, but the car itself had gigantic rear fins and was roughly the size of an aircraft carrier. In that instant, while I stood precariously balanced on that wooden raft with my arms lifted towards the heavens, I thought about dad's ugly car and the fact that I would never live to see fourteen.

When my father saw me standing on that makeshift raft, soaking wet in the middle of that filthy pond, something inside him must have snapped. He jammed the gearshift into park, threw open the door, and jumped out of the car before it had even come to a complete stop. My dad moves fast for a big man. He locked eyes with me across the forty or fifty yards of cattails and pond scum that separated me from his wrath and bellowed, "Richard Glenn Young! What the hell do you think you're doing out there?"

All activity on the pond ceased. The air grew thick and heavy. The frogs and crickets stopped their concert. The cacophony of our collective shrieks and laughter was instantaneously swallowed up in silence like so much light being sucked into a black hole.

"You get your butt home right now and wait for me in the basement," he yelled with his voice still at full throttle. "And I want your clothes and shoes washed out by hand before I get there. And by God they had better be clean!" Then he jumped back into his aircraft carrier and sped away, leaving behind a roostertail of dust and gravel.

As Mitch and I paddled our raft towards the shore, my friends lowered their gaze reverently as if watching a royal funeral barge make its solemn journey down the Nile. To their credit, none of them snickered or laughed as I walked away alone and began the two-mile trek towards home. Two miles was a great distance that day.

When I finally reached my house, I went to the back door

that led directly to our basement and crept downstairs as quickly and as quietly as possible. I didn't want my mom to know I was home because I knew she would start asking a lot of "mother" questions. I went into the laundry room, stripped down to my shorts, and started scrubbing my clothes and shoes in the utility sink. For the next hour or so, I washed and scrubbed and cried. And I waited.

The Gift of Grace

I knew the moment my father returned home because I could hear his heavy footsteps and the thud of his leather-soled wingtips as he walked across the floor above my head. I listened as he walked directly from the front door, across the entire house, and into the kitchen without saying a word to my mother. He opened the kitchen door that led to the basement stairs, and I felt my heart start to pound in my chest.

There were exactly seventeen stairs between the kitchen and the basement. I had counted them a thousand times. I counted them now as dad started walking slowly downward. One . . . two . . . three. Every step seemed to take forever as I turned quickly to make sure my jeans and T-shirt were laid out as neatly as possible on the counter. Four . . . five . . . six. I tried to gauge his mood by the sound and rhythm of his approach. His steps were slow and steady and betrayed nothing. Seven . . . eight . . . nine. I could feel a terrible tightness growing in the back of my throat. When he got about halfway down the stairs, I lost count and started sobbing softly. My fear was still intense, but now it had been joined by a tremendous feeling of guilt and shame.

I must have been quite a sight when my father finally reached the bottom of the stairs and turned the corner into the utility room. I stood there in front of him with my head bowed and tears streaming down my face. As he walked slowly towards me, I prepared for whatever punishment was to come.

He stopped about five feet away and said, "Come here son."

His voice was slow and gentle. I looked up at him quickly and there was a soft, almost pensive look in his eyes as if he were thinking of a time long ago.

I shuffled forward cautiously, head down and eyes averted, wondering still if I was about to be hit. Instead, he reached out and folded me into his big, strong arms. As I began to sob, he held me close and said, "I think sometimes boys just have to try things out for themselves." Then even softer, "Now get dressed and come upstairs for dinner."

That night the five of us ate dinner together like we always did. The food tasted very good. Nothing more was ever said about my adventure and I never went to the pond again. I never wanted to.

M EDITATION: *Choosing To Forgive*

The Buddha once likened anger and unforgiveness to picking up a burning ember with your bare hands in order to throw it at someone else, all the while being seared and burned by that anger. When Christ was asked by his disciples how many times they should forgive someone, he replied, "Seventy times seven." Even if he meant that literally, that's a lot of forgiveness.

Sit down in your usual place of meditation, in your usual posture. Bring awareness into your body. Let your attention rest easily on the sensations of your physical being—a tingling here or a vibration there. Don't grasp any of these sensations, just be aware of them with gentle attention as they arise and pass away. Feel your arms and legs. Feel your breath. No words, just bare attention.

Reflect on the way that anger makes you feel. As Stephen Levine says in his beautiful book, *A Gradual Awakening,* "Anger comes from pain and goes back to pain." Feel the tightness in your chest and the fire in your belly that is caused by anger and unforgiveness. Be aware of the separation and isolation you feel and the intense desire to do emotional or even physical injury to the object of your anger. Notice the rationalizations that run through your mind. For example,

"My anger is justified. I have been wronged! Now I have to express this anger outwardly or it will give me hives or an ulcer. Besides, I don't want this person thinking they can walk all over me. I need to be assertive. I need to show my wife (boss, friend, family) that I'm strong."

Does any of this really make you feel any better? Feel the chaos that is created in your thoughts by anger. Unforgiveness is like dropping a huge boulder on the still surface of the mind. Then, as soon as the waves quiet down a little, we drop the boulder again. Maybe it's time to try something different. As they say in Alcoholics Anonymous, insanity is doing the same thing over and over while expecting a different result. Harboring anger, expressing anger, being anger—none of these things works to lead us to liberation.

Return your attention to the sensations of your body. Let your breath come easily and naturally and feel yourself opening up once more to the peace and stillness of this moment. Reflect on the qualities of mind that are the opposite of anger, such as forgiveness, love, and emotional warmth. Let these feelings grow and expand in your awareness. Now, remember those who have caused you pain or anger in the past, whether purposefully or accidentally. Think of them by name, if you can. Direct these feelings of warmth and love and forgiveness to each of them individually. Repeat the following words slowly and mindfully as you visualize each of these people in your mind.

I forgive everyone whom I believe has harmed me in the past. I forgive them whether the pain they appeared to inflict upon me was by thought, word, or deed. I forgive them whether their

*actions were intentionally hurtful, thoughtless, or simply acci-
dental. I will no longer hold these things to their account.*

*I ask them now to forgive me for anything I may have done to
cause them pain. I am truly sorry. I send them peace and pray
that they will send me peace in return.*

■

16

A GIFT OF FAITH

If you love only those who love you, what merit is there in that? For even godless people love those who love them. And if you help only those who help you, what merit is there in that? Even godless people act in that way. And if you lend only to people from whom you expect to get something, what merit is there in that? Even godless people lend to godless people, meaning to get it back again in full. But love your enemies, and help them and lend to them, never despairing, and you will be richly rewarded, and you will be sons of the Most High, for He is kind even to the ungrateful and the wicked. You must be merciful, just as your Father is.

JESUS THE CHRIST

By our love for other men, we enable them to discover Christ in themselves and to pass through Christ to the Source, the Beginning of all life, the Father, present and hidden in the depths of their own being. Finding Him, they who have long been torn and divided by the disintegrating force of their own illusions are able to discover and integrate themselves in One.

THOMAS MERTON

DURING my high school years, my family and I were members of Columbia Heights Baptist Church in Longview, Washington. Longview was a quiet little lumber and paper mill town with a population of about 30,000.

In spite of its relatively small size, Longview boasted five different Baptist churches. It seems Baptists really like to "cuss and discuss" theological issues and this propensity towards divine debate has a tendency to split churches. The result is that new Baptist churches are constantly being established within the same community. This makes it possible for the disgruntled members of the old church to go and start a new church. It's a strange method of evangelism and church expansion, I know, but it seems to work for Baptists.

Hence my parents' confusion and mild disapproval when I told them I wanted to begin attending First Baptist Church. This was the largest Baptist church in town. It was located on a prime piece of real estate, just across from the lake and next to the community hospital. All of the smaller Baptist churches had sprung from this one in years gone by for reasons nobody could quite remember and there were still some feelings of righteous indignation and envy towards "First Church" in the greater Baptist community.

I wanted to attend First Baptist for a couple of reasons. First, in my junior year of high school, I had auditioned and been accepted into the "Lower Columbia Singers." This was a very popular, community-based youth choir that toured all over the country and was sponsored in large part by First Baptist. Second, and more to the point, I was extremely interested in a certain young lady with marvelous blonde hair and blue eyes who attended that church and who was also the accompanist for the "Singers." These seemed to me like two very good reasons, bordering on a divine mandate, for switching churches. I'm sure God completely understood this hormonal imperative even if my parents did not. So during my senior year at R.A. Long High School and then my first year at Lower Columbia College, I became a very active part of the youth program at First Baptist.

In June of 1971, after I had completed a rather lackluster first year in junior college, my girlfriend (the one with the hair and eyes) decided to go on a one-week vacation with the director of the Singers and his family to Southern California. The director's name was Ted Campbell, and he and his wife Betty were a very influential part of our lives at that time. They were also alumni of California Baptist College in Riverside, California, and were very interested in getting my girlfriend to attend their alma mater. I was very interested in keeping her in Longview.

I had decided Nancy was the girl I wanted to marry, and I had no intentions of leaving our fair city. Needless to say, I didn't want her to go on this trip. But no amount of whimpering or whining on my part could change her mind about going on this vacation to Sodom and Gomorrah. I even tried simulating a major physical disorder. Nothing worked. She remained steadfast and unmoved in her decision to investigate the college. Years later I would refer to this quality of hers as stubbornness. I remember watching Ted's stuffed-to-the-gills, blue Volkswagen van drive out of sight on that early summer morning. I had the uncomfortable feeling my secure world was about to be turned upside down.

When Nancy returned one week later, she could speak of nothing else except California Baptist College. She talked endlessly about the beauty of the campus and about all of the wonderful people she had met while she was there. She told me about palm trees and warm summer breezes, Disneyland and the California beaches (she failed to mention anything about SMOG). She even tried to convince me it would be a good thing for her to go away to college so she could "become independent and find my own identity."

I definitely didn't like the sound of that, so I countered by purchasing an engagement ring. I gave it to her one night in the front seat of my 1965 Pontiac LeMans while we were parked in front of her house. She accepted the ring and my proposal of marriage but said she was still going to California. I tried the whimpering thing again but to no avail.

At this point, I knew I was not going to be able to change her decision. So I did the only rational thing I could under the circumstances: I started to make plans to go with her. I had to go. I had no choice. She was going to need my protection and the benefit of my greater wisdom and experience in the world. After all, I was a year older than she.

There were only a couple of small problems with this entirely noble plan. For one thing, I had no money for a private college and no idea how I was going to get it. I was just getting by on the paycheck of a grocery store boxboy, and my parents certainly couldn't afford to send me away to school. The deadline for applications for the fall semester at CBC also had long since passed. But I went forward undaunted despite these dilemmas. In fact, as the weeks wore on, I became absolutely convinced it was God's will for me to attend California Baptist College. I was certain He had a "special ministry" waiting for me as I followed Nancy to the far side of the moon. Does God work in mysterious ways or what?

I look back now on that time in my life with a certain amount of wry amusement. I remember how full I was of equal portions of youthful arrogance and naivete. Yet underneath all the bravado and the proud assertions I made to my friends and family about "God's will," I was very frightened. I was moving a thousand miles away from home to attend a college I knew little or nothing about. I wasn't even sure if the school would accept me since I had failed to apply before the deadline for the fall semester. I had no money, no job, and no ideas. I had nothing but an adolescent's beginning faith in God and a fiancee who loved me. In fear and trembling, I began my preparations to leave. Little did I know there were others who were making preparations as well.

Elmer Jones was a successful engineer at one of the mills in Longview and chairman of the board of deacons at First Baptist Church. He was always a rather imposing figure to me. In addition to his many duties as head deacon, he sang bass every Sunday morning and evening in the church choir. Elmer had a very powerful and distinctive voice that seemed to fit his tall, lanky, midwestern farmer's physique. He always sang with tremendous energy and enthusiasm, even though he was often a bit off key. Of course, no one really minded Elmer's lack of perfect pitch because he so obviously enjoyed what he was doing.

We also didn't mind that he sat on the back row of the choir loft every Superbowl Sunday with a transistor radio in his pocket and an earphone snaking up through the collar of his white shirt. That was just Elmer's way. I do wish, though, he would have flashed the score to the rest of us poor souls in the congregation instead of just sitting there with that big smile on his face.

It happened on a particularly balmy Sunday evening after church, about three weeks before Nancy and I were scheduled to leave for California. I had not yet been accepted at CBC and had no idea how I was going to pay for it, but I was still determined to go. Just as I was getting into my car in the parking lot, I heard Elmer's deep voice call me from the back door of the church. "Hey Rich, could I talk to you for a minute?"

I must admit that I was a taken aback by this greeting. In the two years I had known him, Elmer had never done more than smile and nod his head in my direction. I knew he and his wife were good friends of Nancy's parents, but I couldn't imagine what business he could possibly have with me. I tried to remember if I had done anything wrong around the church that could have come to his attention.

Guilt is indigenous to Baptist adolescents, especially when confronted by a head deacon. Maybe I had peeled out of the parking lot a little too energetically that morning after services. That must be it. He'd probably seen me pull out and wanted to remind me to take it easy.

I watched as Elmer shook one last hand and headed in my direction, his long legs devouring the distance between us. I quickly prepared my feeble defense and my best apology. As he came around the side of my car, I took his proffered hand and felt the great strength in his grip. "I hear you're planning to go to California Baptist College in the next few weeks, Rich, is that right?" His voice was surprisingly soft, almost timid.

"Yes sir, that's right," I said, a little uncertainly. I was surprised by Elmer's question and by his slightly self-conscious manner.

"Well . . . I also heard you're a little unsure of how you're going to pay for all of your expenses down there."

At this point, I had no idea what Elmer was trying to say or how I should respond. Should I tell him the truth about my fears or give him the same pat answers I had been giving to my family and friends over the past several weeks about trusting God and hoping for a scholarship or a job? Before I could reply, he hurried on. "Barbara and I have been putting away a little money over the past couple of years. We now have the opportunity to invest in some vacation property on the Toutle River or to invest in your future. We've decided to invest in you."

It took a couple extra seconds for his words to register in my brain. Did he just say something about investing in my future? No, I must have heard him wrong. My heart began to beat faster as I waited for him to continue.

"Here's what we would like to do, Rich. We will pay for all of your college expenses including tuition, books, room and board, and a little spending money . . . everything you will need for the next four years."

I couldn't believe what I was hearing. I managed to say in a voice no louder than a whisper, "You want to pay for everything?"

"Yes, we do, Rich." His voice was much more confident now. "We will consider this a no-interest loan; and when you graduate, you can pay us back in whatever monthly installments you can afford. But there is one thing I will ask you to do in return."

"Yes, sir?"

"I want you to promise me someday you will do the same thing for someone else."

"Yes sir, I will. I promise."

There is absolutely no way I can convey how stunned I felt at that moment. A man I barely knew was offering to pay for my entire college education. I was completely mystified by Elmer's enormous generosity and his apparent faith in my potential.

I'm sure I must have mumbled my thanks. I really don't remember exactly what I said. I do know I was working hard to control the ocean-swell of emotions inside.

As he turned to go, Elmer suggested that I give him a call sometime during the week so we could get together and work out a budget for the first semester. He quickly jotted down his home phone number on the back of a business card and handed it to me. Then he smiled softly and walked away.

The following Saturday, I gathered what little information I had about Cal Baptist and went over to Elmer and Barbara's house. Elmer and I sat alone in the dining room while Barbara and the kids busied themselves elsewhere. We spent about two hours figuring out a tentative budget for the fall semester. When we were finished and it was time for me to go, he handed me a check for eleven hundred dollars. That was enough to cover all of my school and living expenses until the spring. We agreed to meet during Christmas vacation to plan for the rest of the school year.

I was extremely grateful for the money and told Elmer so at least twenty times. But I had no idea what I had really just been given. I left the Jones' home that day with something far more valuable than money. For reasons known only to himself, Elmer believed in my potential even though he hardly knew me. He had faith in my future and was willing to help pay for it, even though he had three children of his own to educate. What an inestimable gift that was to a frightened and insecure eighteen-year-old boy. I left for college two weeks later with Elmer's check in my pocket. But more importantly, I left with Elmer's blessing on my life.

A couple of days after my arrival at the front door of California Baptist College, my application for the fall semester was approved and I started classes as a second-semester freshman. Shortly after that, I auditioned for and received a generous vocal music scholarship that paid for most of my college tuition for the next four years. I also got a job as a grocery clerk that helped pay for books and living expenses. So after that first semester, it wasn't necessary for Elmer to loan me any more money. God does indeed work in mysterious ways.

After I graduated from CBC and started on my master's degree at Cal State, Fullerton, my father went to Elmer to make arrangements to repay my loan. Elmer told my father he wanted me to consider the eleven hundred dollars a gift. He didn't want to be repaid, but he did want me to remember the promise I had made about helping someone else with their education. I did remember. I considered it a sacred oath.

In the fall of 1995, I received word through Nancy's parents that Elmer Jones had died at the age of fifty-nine of a massive heart attack. I was shocked when I first heard the news and then I felt a great sadness. He was much too young and vital to be taken in such a way. I can only imagine the sorrow and emptiness his family and friends must have felt at his passing. I know the sorrow I felt.

There were no words of comfort, no tribute, that could suffice to ease the pain for those who knew and loved him. Only time could do that and then only imperfectly. I just knew this. Elmer Jones taught me about love and generosity and faith in the young. He showed me the face of Christ, real and honest, rugged and hopeful, each time I looked into his face. He gave me a gift that has shaped the course of my entire life. He showed me how to believe in myself, which is always the first step on the journey Home.

I won't forget you, Elmer. And I won't forget my promise.

17

MYSTICAL WISDOM

The dogmas and creeds with which the term "Christianity" be-
came finally associated in its ecclesiastical hierarchical form
were the result of an intense struggle between an original mys-
tical and esoteric Christology, known to and taught by men
who were more or less familiar with the Ancient Wisdom, and
another set of men who were crude realists, literalists, and
historicizers of the mystical allegories—commencing with the
first chapter of Genesis. If the Garden of Eden story could be
taken by these as literal history, can we be surprised at the
dogmas which they subsequently based thereon?

WILLIAM KINGSLAND

We are not suggesting that the literal interpretation of the Faith
should be replaced by a mystical interpretation, but that the
mystical must come out of the literal and exist in addition to it.
Granting all those events and all the claims which the Church
makes for Christ to be factually true, they are still symbols.
They are symbolic events revealing the nature of God and the
way in which man realizes union with God.

ALAN WATTS

THE PROTESTANT tradition in which I was raised emphasized
the literal (exoteric) interpretation of scripture and made no
bones about it. We were expected to believe the earth was

created in six twenty-four-hour periods of time (He rested on the seventh) and Jonah really lived in the belly of a whale for three days. It was also hinted at in some quarters that dinosaur bones were planted on earth by the Devil in order to undermine our faith in the biblical account of creation, since dinosaurs aren't mentioned anywhere in the scriptures. No, I'm not kidding.

Symbolic or metaphorical (esoteric) interpretations were simply not allowed. If you couldn't believe everything in the Bible was factually true and historically accurate to the last detail, then how could you know any of it was true? Failure to accept this basic theological premise was considered to be the result of a severe lack of faith in God or too much humanistic education.

I think I was in high school when I first noticed that scientific "facts" were always changing, depending upon who was interpreting them and at what point in time. In my physics class, for example, we were taught that electrons rotate around the nucleus of an atom in very predictable orbits, like mini-planets around a microscopic sun. That was a fact. If you didn't believe it, you flunked the test. Simple enough. Today they teach you can never really know where an electron will end up from one moment to the next: something about the "uncertainty principle." Now that is the fact. Okay. So change your answer on the exam. But which "fact" is really the fact? Do we know what electrons are going to do or not?

It wasn't long before I noticed the same phenomenon in regards to biblical facts. Wasn't it only a few hundred years ago when we arrested people and consigned them to the fires of hell for refusing to accept the "fact" that the sun and planets rotate around the earth? After all, the Church had proven conclusively by use of the Bible that the earth was the center of the universe. I think it was Galileo who flunked that exam.

I was also in high school when I noticed certain things could be overflowing with Truth and not be the least bit factual—like the story of Cinderella or the Prodigal Son. Conversely, there were many things which were completely factual and yet were all but useless in helping me understand the deeper truths of my existence—like yesterday's baseball scores.

I was confused and perhaps a bit frightened by my observation that the "facts" and the "truth" are capable of being quite independent of each other. For example, I couldn't figure out what difference it could possibly make to the truth of God's creative energy if the earth evolved in seven geologic periods, each lasting several million years, or was created in seven days. And did it really matter that Buddha was enlightened under a Bodhi tree? Wouldn't it have worked just as well under a spreading chestnut? But I was a good Baptist boy, and didn't talk about these things in polite company.

Imagine my dilemma several years ago when I started reading the mystical literature of several different religious traditions, including Christianity. All of a sudden I was exposed to the lives of vital and saintly men and women who looked at everything from a symbolic and metaphorical perspective. They seemed to believe historical facts were secondary to the Truth being expressed at a much deeper level. I also became aware that the experience of Truth they each tried to describe remained fundamentally and universally the same for all of them. It didn't matter what the facts were about their religious orientation, their language, their time in history, or their particular method of contemplation or meditation. They each spoke of the same ineffable Reality in similar ways.

I have mentioned Meister Eckhart before. He was the thirteenth-century Dominican priest and spiritual director who stands at the pinnacle of mystical wisdom in the Western world. You gotta love a guy who was condemned by the enlightened literalists of his day, the Spanish Inquisitors. I'll never forget when I tried to read one of his sermons for the first time. He was preaching on a passage of scripture with which I was very familiar, but I couldn't follow his exegesis to save my life. I had absolutely no idea what this man was trying to say. I know now this confusion was due to my ignorance of Eckhart's esoteric method of interpretation. Like every good mystic, he would dig under the surface of words and apparent meanings to find the Truth which lies hidden in the depths of the scriptures and within the sanctuary of our own souls.

What follows is something similar. I have interpreted an event from the life of Abraham in an esoteric fashion and tried to relate this truth to the final goal of the mystical journey—transformation of consciousness and union with God. I am not attempting to undermine the historicity of this story or to detract in any way from the more traditional or orthodox interpretations of its meaning. I only wish to offer an example of the deeper, more universal truths which can be mined from the scriptures of any religious tradition regarding the process of spiritual regeneration.

Abraham, Isaac & Egos

The first passage is taken from the fifteenth chapter of the book of Genesis and begins to detail an important series of events in the lives of Abraham and Sarah Goldstein (okay, so we don't really know their last name). Abraham is important as a mythical as well as historical figure because he is venerated as the "father" of all three of the world's monotheistic religions: Judaism, Christianity, and Islam. This endows the events of his life with a deeply symbolic importance that must be appreciated if we are to fully understand the spiritual journey as it is practiced in each of these three faiths.

Because of Abraham's unique position in history, his life can be seen as a mystical allegory that is deeply imbedded in the collective unconscious of all monotheistic religions. His willingness to leave everything behind and journey from his secure home in Ur of the Chaldees (which symbolically represents our normal state of consciousness) to the unknown country of Hebron (enlightened consciousness) at the internal urging of God, his decision to have a child by the handmaid Hagar instead of waiting for the child of promise to be born of Sarah, and then his supreme willingness to sacrifice the life of his precious son Isaac on the altar of God—all these events are symbolic of spiritual stages we must successfully negotiate on our journey Home.

When interpreted literally and historically, Abraham's life is an inspiring example of faith and obedience to God. When examined esoterically, his words and decisions and adventures provide a powerful psychological map of the inner territory of our own psyche that we must traverse in order to return to the awareness of our true Selves. Let's pick up the action just outside of Hebron.

> *And Abram said, "O Lord God, what wilt Thou give me, since I am childless, and the heir of my house is Eliezer of Damascus? Since Thou hast given no offspring to me, one born in my house is my heir." Then behold, the word of the Lord came to him saying, "This man will not be your heir; but one who shall come forth from your body, he shall be your heir." And he took him outside and said, "Now look toward the heavens, and count the stars, if you are able to count them. So shall your descendants be." Then he believed in the Lord; and He reckoned it to him as righteousness.*[1]

God spoke to Abram and said he and his wife, Sarai, would conceive and give birth to a child: a child of promise, a miraculous child who would be a blessing to all nations forever. At the factual and historical level of interpretation, this promise referred quite literally to the birth of Isaac. At a slightly deeper level, this event was meant to be symbolic of the eventual coming of Jesus Christ, God's miraculous child of promise, into human history. But at the deepest and most mystical level of interpretation, God was speaking to Abram directly in his soul about the birth of the Christ child within Abram's own mind. After all, what good is a child of blessing if that child lacks the power to transform us? God was promising Abram the gift of transformation and the attainment of a higher consciousness or understanding of his full identity within the Godhead. And it was a promise God intended to keep.[2]

Eckhart's mystical theology offers some justification for this interpretation. For Eckhart, begetting and giving birth are central and recurrent themes. According to Eckhart's vision, God is eternally in the process of conceiving and giving birth to His Son within our minds. In fact, the very root of His divinity is this ability to give birth to a higher consciousness within us. Ours is a fertile God who is forever bringing Himself/Herself to term in our hearts and minds and experience. As Eckhart says in one of his most famous sermons,

Here in time we make holiday because the eternal birth which God the Father bore and bears unceasingly in eternity is now born in time, in human nature. St Augustine says this birth is always happening. But if it happen not in me what does it profit me? What matters is that it shall happen in me.

We intend therefore to speak of this birth as taking place in us: as being consummated in the virtuous soul; for it is in the perfect soul that God speaks his Word.[3]

In this passage, Eckhart implies as true sons and daughters of God, we too must share in this divine nature. Elsewhere he wrote, "A good person born of goodness and in God enters into all the properties of the divine nature."[4] We can find this same metaphor of giving birth to the divine consciousness in the Buddhist tradition. As Thich Nhat Hanh writes,

The Buddha described the seed of mindfulness that is in each of us as the "womb of the Buddha" (tathagatagarbha). We are all mothers of the Buddha because we are all pregnant with the potential for awakening. If we know how to take care of our baby Buddha by practicing mindfulness in our daily lives, one day the Enlightened One will reveal himself or herself in us.[5]

If it is true we are children of God and share completely in His divine essence, then our divinity demands that we too become creators through the continual practice of recollection and mindfulness. Such practice enables us to conceive and nourish a profoundly peaceful and abiding Presence within the depths of our own being.

The Orthodox Heresy

The truest indication we have become children of God is when we give birth to the Christ Child, the Logos or Divine Word, which God is continually conceiving within us and speaking in our hearts. Our highest calling is to bring "to term" the Christ/ Buddha/Krishna/Muhammad Consciousness that lies dormant within our own minds and allow it to transform our lives and relationships. This is exactly what Jesus meant when he said, "You must be born again." He did not mean we must intellec- tually agree to a particular body of doctrines or religious prac- tices that are loosely based on accrued, idiosyncratic human interpretations of his life and ministry. There was no "Christian Doctrine" when Christ called us to wake up and rediscover our true nature. This is all so much intellectual and linguistic double-talk which serves only to separate us further from our Divine Source. Nor did he expect we would begin to divide ourselves into warring factions based on totally irrelevant issues such as whether we should go to church on Saturday or Sunday or even whether Jews and Arabs worship the same God.

It is time for all of us—Christians, Jews, and Muslims alike— to admit that for the past several hundred years our institution- alized religions have given us a totally inadequate definition and understanding of the profound transformation of con- sciousness that constitutes true salvation. We have not been taught how to meet God directly within the deepest part of our own minds. We have been taught instead that following the ecclesiastical rules and participating in the institutional sacra- ments will enable us to fulfill our highest religious aspirations.

Anyone who has done this for any length of time knows it is simply not true. Without the vital message of mystical transfor- mation and spiritual freedom, religion eventually becomes just another institutional responsibility that demands our time and energy. Sooner or later, most people will simply lose interest. Then they either leave the organized Church altogether or join a more loosely organized group that promises some kind of pseudo-mystical or emotional experience. The frequent excesses of such groups only serve to increase the gap between orthodoxy and genuine mystical attainment.

There are other, more disturbing changes which occur in the institutions of religious orthodoxy whenever mystic awareness is systematically suppressed or denied. First the mainline (theologically moderate) churches in each of the monotheistic religions stop taking spiritual chances. We learn to play it safe so as not to offend the delicate sensibilities of our religious ego. Then we justify our lack of spiritual courage and innovation by reinterpreting the revolutionary message of our particular Avatar in more socially conventional terms. This may take some doing, since every Avatar has been viewed as a religious radical by the societies to which they were sent.

As a result of this "conventionalization" of the gospel, our moderate churches become routinized and uninspiring places filled with beautiful symbols and grand ceremonies which become ends in themselves. The liturgy becomes a kind of weekly entertainment which no longer serves its original purpose of pointing us in the direction of divine revelation and individual enlightenment. In every culture, orthodoxy begins to lose touch sooner or later with the radical message of the "Gospel of Transformation" which is always *passionate, intellectually intriguing,* and *spiritually challenging.* In place of spiritual awakening, we begin to substitute either misguided emotionalism or social concern and political activism. While these latter activities are vital for every religion to initiate and nurture, such efforts can only be effective in changing and improving the lives of others when they are guided by those individuals who have first awakened to the unity of all life.

There is a second problem which can occur when we stop initiating believers into the deeper mysteries of religious faith and start discouraging them from trying to find their own unique experience of God. We may start believing all scripture must be literally and historically accurate in order to be true. This is a serious mistake (which seems to primarily plague the monotheistic religions) and I think it happens for a couple of reasons.

For one thing, it gives the ego a greater sense of control because literalization of truth makes it easier to create rules and regulations for virtually every situation in life. This can help us to feel safer and can also provide the ego with a marvelous tool for judging others, thereby maintaining its illusion of separate existence. Ask any Pharisee.

In addition, the literalization and codification of spiritual teachings may be a conservative backlash to what is seen as the lifeless ritual and liberal orientation of many mainline churches. But instead of solving the real problem of "tired orthodoxy" by welcoming and pursuing mystical intuition and transformation, we substitute a misplaced and often fanatical passion for the concrete written revelation of scripture.

Religious beliefs and dogma can become distorted and even dangerous as the result of continual emphasis on the concrete and literal interpretations of God's various Self-revelations throughout human history. This literalization of the Word of God—whether it be found in the Bible, the Koran, or the Torah—always leads to the same frightening excesses of religious fundamentalism and racism. It destroys the Truth by insisting everything must be "factual and historical." And sooner or later, when fundamentalism has run its logical course, hundreds or even thousands of our innocent brothers and sisters in various parts of the world are systematically persecuted and/ or annihilated in the name of God or a particular religious sect. Today it is happening in Bosnia. Just yesterday it happened in Nazi Germany and Russia.

Love which is not continually nourished by mystical knowledge and spiritual transformation can become sick and twisted to the point that religious dedication is defined as absolute obedience to a god who demands strict adherence to the letter of the law, however it is defined by a particular group. We will then project from the dark recesses of our own unexplored minds an image of a god who judges swiftly (just as we do) and who exacts tremendous punishment when there is the slightest disobedience among his followers. It is a small step then to becoming the instruments of that divine wrath ourselves.

Let there be no mistake. This has never been the message of any of the Avatars sent into the world to help us awaken to our original identity. Their message is always the same and always universal: a message of unconditional grace and love, mutual tolerance, tenacious forgiveness, and the realization of unity and oneness with our brothers and with all of creation. Any other teaching than this is a fearful distortion perpetrated upon the human race by the machinations of the separated and frightened ego in its endless search for a feeling of safety and righteousness.

I would venture to say the increasing worldwide trend we are now observing in terrorism, religious rioting, racial hatred, and holy wars is directly related to the rise of crude realism, scriptural historicizing, and theological literalism among the leaders and scholars of the monotheistic religions. Combine this with the systematic suppression and persecution of all forms of mysticism and the Ancient Wisdom, beginning with the Christian Gnostics in the second century, and you have all the elements necessary for the Crusades.

Christ said we must be born again of the Spirit. Buddha said the same thing utilizing a different metaphor which was more suited to the needs and understanding of his culture and time in history. He said we are all asleep in the midst of a painful dream and must awaken to our true identity. Different metaphors speak in different ways to different peoples about the same spiritual realities.

But let's stick with the metaphor Christ used. In essence, he said we must give birth to the divine Child within our hearts. We ourselves must become mothers of God, birthers of the Child of God in our transformed minds and hearts and into human history. This is the truest measure of our fruitfulness and of our "new birth." It is also a much harder truth to actualize in our experience than simply "accepting Jesus Christ as our personal Lord and Savior."

Anyone can agree to accept the intellectual and emotional teachings of the Church concerning Christ, his ministry on earth, his role as the supreme sacrifice for sin, and his position of authority and Lordship in the life of the believer. But this is not salvation or enlightenment. It is only the first step. It does very little to transform our minds or enable us to transcend the pain and suffering "human flesh is heir to." As Christ himself once said, "Many are called but few are chosen." The call of salvation, which is the universal call of the Logos, is to become fully enlightened beings and to live every moment of our lives in conscious unity with God. Anything less is painful and unfulfilling. Anything less is simply not salvation.[6]

The Magnificat of Stillness

So, God comes to Abram and says, "You haven't been able to have a child on your own by natural means (in other words, your ego has failed miserably to provide you with lasting peace). So now there is room for me to move with mystery. I will beget a child within you and you will bear him for me. And he will be a blessing to you and all the nations forever."

In fact, God had this same conversation with Mary several hundred years later. And if the truth be known, He has it with all of us continually in our souls. But how does one give birth to Christ in the world? And why does enlightenment take so long and seem so difficult for the human mind to attain? What is it that so painfully prolongs our "labor?" Let me quote Eckhart's poignant answer to these questions.

So long as you have sorrow in your heart for anything, even for sin, your child will not be born. Do you have sorrow in your heart? Then you are not yet a "mother"; you are rather still in the act of bearing a child and close to the time of birth. On this

*account, however, do not rush into doubt if you are sorrowful
about yourself or a friend of yours. If the child is still not yet
born, it is close to the time of birth. But it is completely born
when a person feels no sorrow in his or her heart. For that person has the essence and nature and substance and wisdom and
joy and everything that God has.[7]*

The continual state of anxiety and fear, guilt and anger born
of the ego's insane belief in separation is what prolongs our
labor and prevents the transformation of consciousness that is
the birth of Christ in our souls. When our minds are running
here and there like wild monkeys in a cage, worrying about this
potential problem and frightened about that painful consequence, it is impossible for us to recollect ourselves sufficiently
to hear the Spirit of God speaking in our hearts. Somehow we
must learn to quiet our fears, let go of the sorrows of everyday
living, and gradually detach ourselves from the little self we
think we are. Only then will we be begin to realize we are the
owners of a vast estate who have been content to live in a tiny
little corner of the potter's field.

The Apostle Paul once wrote, "Let this mind be in you that
was also in Christ Jesus."[8] As we learn to quiet ourselves with
ever increasing regularity and concentration through the practice of detachment and meditation, the mind ripens and is
prepared for its transformation, its epiphany. And when that
moment finally arrives, we will be filled with such an unbelievable sense of peace and freedom that mere words will
never suffice to express it. It matters not whether we call this
experience salvation, enlightenment, satori, kensho, cosmic
consciousness, the mind of Christ, or any other of a dozen
words and phrases. It is quite simply our highest calling, our
deepest longing, and our greatest joy! As Phillip Kapleau writes,

*Such extraordinary happiness makes you realize (among so
many other things) how truly unhappy you had been before.
Not in the life circumstances but in your self, your miserable,
restless, eternally dissatisfied self. This joy is the joy of*

dropping burdens, burdens you didn't even know you had—so deeply had they entered you—dragging you down, grinding you down, making you weigh heavy as lead, move as sluggishly as thick cold molasses.[9]

God has already conceived his Son within each of our minds. The time of birth is at hand. The moment of dawn is almost upon us. Let us free ourselves from any fears about the future and any regrets about the past and wait patiently for the birth of a new consciousness which will complete our joy. God's promise to us is the same He made to Abram. The child (transformed consciousness) *will be* born, and it *will be* a blessing to us and to all nations forever. The time of our awakening, our new birth, was already established before we heard the call and set our foot to the path and nothing in heaven or on earth can prevent it from occurring.

Religious Projects of the Ego

Now, as we return to the story of Abram, we find he accepted God's promises and assurances and began to wait patiently for the moment of fulfillment to arrive. But it wasn't long before Sarai came to him with a truly brilliant idea (esoterically, Sarai represents the feminine, intuitive, right-brained part of Abram). She decided Abram should have a child with Hagar, her handmaiden.

Now Sarai, Abram's wife, had borne him no children, and she had an Egyptian maid whose name was Hagar. So Sarai said to Abram, "Now behold, the Lord has prevented me from bearing children. Please go in to my maid; perhaps I shall obtain children through her." And Abram listened to the voice of Sarai.[10]

Patience is an essential part of the spiritual journey. In one sense, our transformation is already complete and all we really lack is the awareness of our true condition of union with God. But from the perspective of the ego, the process of giving birth to the Christ Consciousness seems to take forever. Abram and

Sarai didn't like waiting. They decided to give birth to the child
their own way. They were looking for a good ego project and
they found it in Hagar.

Sometimes, like Abram and Sarai, we can become impatient
with I AM's sense of timing. So the ego decides to take matters
into its own hands and help God along. As a result, we dive
even deeper into the ego project (our child by Hagar) we may
have modified previously or even left behind in an attempt to
follow God's promise of higher wisdom. We come up with a
wonderful plan, a course of action which is guaranteed to fulfill
all of our spiritual needs and equip us to minister to the rest of
the world. Right. Herein lies the seeds of tremendous egoism.
Paul Brunton points this out when he writes,

> *In the very act of praising God or lauding Spirit, the ego praises
> or lauds itself—such is the cunning duplicity with which it
> leads a man into thinking that he is being very spiritual or
> becoming very pious. . . . The ego can effect tremendous
> achievements in the domain of worldly life but it can do noth-
> ing in the domain of spiritual life. Here its best and only
> achievement is to stop its efforts, silence itself, and learn to
> be still.*[11]

I can only imagine how Abram tried to reason this thing out
in his own mind: "Okay, God promised me a son (read: higher
consciousness) and I believe He meant what He said. But I've
been waiting a long time now and Sarai isn't getting any
younger and for that matter, neither am I. At this rate, I'll have
to go to the kid's Little League games in a wheelchair. Now Sarai
wants me to sleep with Hagar, who, by the way, is not entirely
unattractive, and have a child by her. This sounds crazy to me
but Sarai has always been a practical and level-headed woman.
You know, maybe she's right. I'll bet this is what God had in
mind all along when He promised me a son. He just wanted me
to figure it out for myself!" Beep! Wrong answer, but thank you
for playing our game!

So Abram went in to Hagar and she conceived a child by

him. Hagar symbolically represents all of the things we do to try and transform our own consciousness through the effort of ego. This can include anything capable of focusing attention or altering mood (i.e., drugs, alcohol, overwork, overexercise, music, art, sex, fantasy). The "Hagar" in our lives can also be an activity so time-consuming and all-absorbing we are forced to forget about our "selves" and are thereby able to leave behind the pain of self-awareness, at least for a moment.

The problem with this "Long Path" approach to transformation is, of course, it is always temporary, it is often strenuous, and we constantly have to "up the dosage." It requires we work exceptionally hard for the slim promise of spiritual or emotional release. So we work diligently to improve our ego projects so everyone will be proud and God may grant us some measure of wisdom and happiness. But as God doesn't make these kinds of deals, we are always left empty-handed in the end. As Alan Watts writes,

> *It is generally agreed that happiness cannot be had by any form of direct striving. Like your shadow, the more you chase it, the more it runs away. It is not surprising therefore that in both ancient religions and modern psychology man is advised to relax his self-assertive efforts and acquire a certain passivity of soul, encouraging thereby a state of receptivity or acceptance, which Christianity would describe as easing-up the tumult of self-will in order that it may give place to the will of God. It is as if man were to empty his soul in order that the gifts of the spirit might pour in, on the principle that nature abhors a vacuum. But whether it is called the giving-up of self, submitting to the will of God, accepting life, releasing the tension of striving for happiness or letting oneself go with the stream of life, the essential principle is one of relaxation.*[12]

Obviously, things were not too relaxed in Hebron after this little tête-à-tête between Abram and Hagar. As soon as Hagar got pregnant, she started treating her mistress Sarai with a certain amount of disdain and began to assert her own power within the camp. This is how it always is when we engage in the mad pursuit of ego satisfaction instead of just waiting on God to do the thing He has absolutely promised to do. Projects always seem like such a great idea at the time. They feel good and even fulfilling at first, but soon they begin to control our lives addictively just like Hagar tried to control Sarai's and Abram's. But eventually the ego project blows up in our face and causes no end to pain and sorrow for ourselves and all those we love. That is, if we're lucky it does.

Detaching From the Project

When Sarai had taken just about all of this she was going to take, she went to Abram and complained. He did the wise, husbandly thing and said, "Do whatever you want, dear." So Sarai started to treat Hagar harshly. This symbolizes our initial insight into the futility of ego projects, especially religious ones, and our first clumsy attempts to push schemes of the ego away. This is good. In fact, it is a necessary step on the journey. We become disgusted with the compulsive power of our project and we resolve to become free of its influence. But as we will see in a moment, nothing is wasted as we move forward on the path of salvation. Projects don't get destroyed. They get transformed.

Hagar, frightened by her mistress' sudden show of power, fled into the desert. God stopped her on the way and told her to return to Sarai and submit to her authority. Even though Hagar was not the vessel of blessing God intended to use in the life of Abram, He still pronounced a traditional blessing upon her and her descendants forever.

Now the angel of the Lord found her by a spring of water in the wilderness, by the spring on the way to Shur. And he said, "Hagar, Sarai's maid, where have you come from and where are you going?" And she said, "I am fleeing from the presence of my mistress Sarai." Then the angel of the Lord said to her, "Return to your mistress and submit yourself to her authority."

Moreover, the angel said to her, "I will greatly multiply your descendants so that they will be too many to count."[13]

In the very same way, I AM intercepts us just as the mad pursuit of our ego project and its demand for increasing effort threatens to drive us into the desert of despair. Finding us thirsty and hopeless, He pronounces a blessing upon us and upon our project forever and then proceeds to use that same project in a way that is consistent with His purpose for our lives. In essence, God transforms our self-inflicted curse into a gift of grace which enables us to make the transition from Long Path *doing* to Short Path *living* and moves us further along the road to transformation. As the Apostle Paul once said, "All things work together for good for them that love the Lord and are called according to His purpose."[14]

So, did Abram make a mistake with Hagar? Do our ego projects and silly attempts at self-transformation lead us astray? The answer is, "Yes and no." Abram did indeed take the promise of God into his own hands. He did try to give birth to the child in his own heart through his own means and this created no end of troubles for him. But the good news here, and it is really good, is in God's economy there are no mistakes. There are only lessons. Nothing we can do today, no matter how stupid or destructive, can prevent or even prolong the moment of our awakening. This is the ultimate purpose and promise of unconditional Grace. And this is the Good News the Logos speaks forever in our hearts.

Our view of time is linear; God's is not. For I AM, everything we call past, present, and future, is eternally NOW. Since He knows NOW what kind of ego nonsense we're going to pull ten years from our linear present, He makes provision NOW so the consequences of that action will fit perfectly into His plan for our lives, in which He is intimately present.

We Are the Tao

I AM's presence in our lives is so complete, so all-embracing, it is no longer our life at all. In fact, it never was. Whether we admit it or not, it is His life we lead. Our experiences of joy and pain are I AM's experiences as well, for He dwells in our souls and watches over every aspect of our lives with as much love as if we were His own Self. For indeed, we are. It is I AM's very closeness that makes it difficult for us to verbalize, understand, or even recognize this intimate connection. He is the very life that surges through our veins with every beat of our hearts. With each breath we take, we inhale I AM's grace and divinity. This complete identity and intimacy of our essence with God makes it almost impossible to catch Him in the act as His love works to bring good out of all our mistakes.

There is no such thing as a misstep on the spiritual journey. Yes, we can make it easy on ourselves ("My yoke is easy, my burden is light") or very, very difficult (which is the way I apparently like to do it). But whether we step forwards, backwards, sideways, or stand on our heads according to our perception of things, I AM sees to it that every thought, every deed, every decision leads us inevitably to the moment when we can give birth to the Christ-consciousness, the Christ Child within our minds.

Julian of Norwich, the renowned English mystic, wrote the following words of joyous praise and revelation after a moment of illumination of the Christ-Mind within her.

> *See! I am God. See! I am in everything. See! I never lift my hands off my works, nor will I ever. See! I lead everything toward the purpose for which I ordained it, without beginning, by the same Power, Wisdom and Love by which I created it. How could anything be amiss?*[15]

I AM's grace is irresistible and Its purpose is unfailing. The birth of Christ, the eternal Logos, in our hearts and minds is promised and assured. The moment of our complete liberation has been set since the beginning of time and nothing we can do with our little ego projects could possibly prevent it. The blessing has been pronounced on all the generations of our descendants. Our spiritual heritage is as vast as the numberless stars in the heavens. Everything has already been settled. So spread the good Word the journey Home to our Father/our Self is nearly complete. I can smell the fatted calf roasting on the bar-b-que even now.

AFTERWORD

by Sheldon Z. Kramer, Ph.D.

THE BOOK you have just read is a unique contribution to a growing literature on the integration of psychology, science, and the ancient spiritual traditions. As more and more people are becoming disillusioned with traditional Christian churches and are looking for a deeper spiritual life, Richard Young comes along in a very humane, touching way with the story of his own journey deep into the heart of Jesus Christ's teachings. He leads us to understand these teachings not only through his own life, but through the lives and testimonies of various Christian mystics such as the great Thomas Merton, who has written:

> *The union of the Christian and Christ is not just similarity of inclination and feeling, a mutual consent of minds and wills. It has a more radical, more mysterious and supernatural quality: it is a mystical union in which Christ Himself becomes the source and principle of divine life in me.*[1]

In this moving account of a Christian's journey into wholeness, Richard expands the boundaries of traditional Christian thought and shows how the ancient teachings of Christ are deeply embedded in a greater universal, mystical doctrine of the Oneness of Life that is found in most other religious traditions. Dr. Young compares many of Jesus' teachings with the best of what the perennial philosophy has to teach us about returning to our own heart and rediscovering our true identity. His incredible insight into the unity of Truth allows him to integrate Christian wisdom with other spiritual systems (for example, by comparing meditation methods found in Christian contemplation with Buddhist methods as well as Chinese wisdom).

You will have noticed that Richard also gives very practical information and step-by-step instructions on how to increase our ability to contemplate more effectively, taking the best of different meditation technologies and bringing them into the light of Christian contemplative thought. In so doing, he returns us to the truth that salvation, enlightenment, or awakening is more a process than an event—an ongoing practice that requires time and commitment in addition to a continual faith in and reliance upon Divine Grace.

Paths of a Prodigal is on the cutting edge of a growing body of literature on religious mysticism, alternative medicine, and the universal perennial wisdom. Dr. Young's unique contribution is his ability to bring all of these disparate parts directly into the heart of the Christian tradition. I hope this book has stimulated your own process of spiritual awakening and that it will serve as a catalyst to lead you on to other experiences that will further deepen your understanding and transform your life.

SHELDON Z. KRAMER, PH.D., Director
Institute for Transformations
San Diego, California

NOTES

Preface

Epigraph 1: Sam Keen, *The Passionate Life: Stages of Loving* (San Francisco: Harper & Row, Publishers, 1983), p. 179.

Epigraph 2: *A Course in Miracles: Text* (Tiburon, California: Foundation for Inner Peace, 1985), p. 365.

1. Alan Watts, *The Meaning of Happiness* (New York: Harper & Row, Publishers, 1968), p. 28.

Introduction

Epigraph 1: D.T. Suzuki, *Essays in Zen Buddhism, First Series* (New York: Grove Press, 1961), p. 153.

Epigraph 2: Joseph Campbell, *A Joseph Campbell Companion*, ed. Diane K. Osborn (New York: HarperCollins Publishers, 1991), p. 79.

Chapter 1: *Ego Projects*

Epigraph 1: Soren Kierkegaard, *Journal*, May 12, 1839.

Epigraph 2: Alan Watts, *Talking Zen* (New York: Weatherhill Inc., 1994), p. 155.

1. Ernest Becker, *The Denial of Death* (New York: The Free Press, 1973), p. 26.

2. Erich Fromm, *The Sane Society* (New York: Fawcett Books, 1955), p. 34.

3. Mu-mon, *The Gateless Gate*, trans. Nyogen Sengaki and Paul Reps (New York: Anchor Books, 1989), p. 120.

4. Wes Nisker, *Crazy Wisdom* (Berkeley, California: Ten Speed Press, 1990), p. 3.

Chapter 2: *Dealing With Pain*

Epigraph 1: Soren Kierkegaard, *Fear and Trembling* and *The Sickness Unto Death*, trans. Walter Lowrie (Princeton, New Jersey: Princeton University Press, 1954), p. 129.

Epigraph 2: Paul Brunton, *The Peace Within You*, from volume 15 of *The*

Notebooks of Paul Brunton (New York: Larson Publications, 1988), Part 2, p. 14.

1. The Buddha, quoted in Samuel Bercholz & Sherab Chodzin Kohn, *Entering the Stream: An Introduction to the Buddha and His Teachings* (Boston: Shambhala, 1993), p. 62.

2. Thomas Merton, *No Man Is an Island* (New York: Harcourt Brace Jovanovich, Publishers, 1983), p. 81.

3. James W. Fowler and Sam Keen, *Life Maps: Conversations on the Journey of Faith*, ed. Jerome W. Berryman (Waco, Texas: Word Books Publisher, 1985), p.111.

Chapter 3: *Celebrate Life!*

Epigraph 1: Sue Woodruff, *Meditations with Mechtild of Magdeburg* (Santa Fe, New Mexico: Bear & Co., 1987), p. 47.

Epigraph 2: Alice Miller, *For Your Own Good* (New York: Farrar Straus Giroux, 1984) p. 11.

Chapter 4: *Birdsong*

Epigraph 1: Wolfram von Eschenbach, *Parzwal* 3.118.14–17 and 28; trans. (in part) Helen M. Mustard and Charles E. Passage (New York: Vintage Books, 1961), p. 127.

Epigraph 2: Zen poem, author unknown.

1. Suzuki, *Essays*, p. 244.

Chapter 5: *Laughing at Ourselves*

Epigraph 1: Paul Brunton, *The Ego* and *From Birth to Rebirth*, volume 6 from *The Notebooks of Paul Brunton* (New York: Larson Publications, 1987), Part 1, p. 15.

Epigraph 2: Campbell, *Companion*, p. 20.

1. Jean Houston, quoted in Rick Fields with Peggy Taylor, Rex Weyler & Rick Ingrasci, *Chop Wood, Carry Water* (Los Angeles: Jeremy P. Tarcher, Inc., 1984), p. 146.

Chapter 6: *Knowing the Truth*

Epigraph 1: Alan Watts, *The Supreme Identity* (New York: Vintage Books, 1972), p. 88.

Epigraph 2: Brunton, *Ego*, p. 4.

1. Pat Rodegast and Judith Stanton, eds., *Emmanuel's Book: A Manual for Living Comfortably in the Cosmos* (New York: Bantam Books, 1985), p. 37.

Chapter 7: *Being and Doing*

Epigraph 1: Hubert Benoit, *Zen and the Psychology of Transformation: The Supreme Doctrine* (Rochester, Vermont: Inner Traditions International, 1990), p. 16.

Epigraph 2: *A Course in Miracles: Text*, p. 363.

1. Paul Brunton, *Advanced Contemplation* and *The Peace Within You*, volume 15 in *The Notebooks of Paul Brunton* (New York: Larson Publications, 1988), Part 1, p. 47.

2. Paul Tillich, *The New Being* (New York: Charles Scribner's Sons, 1955), pp. 12–13.

3. *A Course in Miracles: Text*, p. 452.

4. I Peter 5:6–7.

5. *A Course in Miracles: Text*, pp. 549–50.

Chapter 8: *Meditation*

Epigraph 1: Sogyal Rinpoche, *The Tibetan Book of Living and Dying* (New York: HarperCollins Publishers, 1992), p. 57.

Epigraph 2: Charlotte Joko Beck, *Everyday Zen: Love and Work*, ed. Steve Smith (San Francisco: Harper & Row, Publisher, 1989), p.5.

1. Anthony Stevens, *Archetypes: A Natural History of the Self* (New York: William Morrow & Co., 1982), pp. 255–56.

2. Abraham Joshua Heschel, *The Earth is the Lord's* (New York: Farrar Straus Giroux, 1978), pp. 70–71.

3. Armstrong, *History*, p. 397.

4. Rinpoche, *Tibetan Book*, pp. 57–58.

5. Campbell, *Companion*, p. 183.

6. Suzuki, *Essays*, p. 246.

7. John 3:3–8.

8. Joseph Goldstein and Jack Kornfield, *Seeking the Heart of Wisdom: The Path of Insight Meditation* (Boston: Shambhala, 1987), p. 25.

9. Mahatma Gandhi, in Eknath Easwaran, *Meditation: A Simple 8-Point Program for Translating Spiritual Ideals into Daily Life* (Tomales, California: Nilgiri Press, 1991), p. 62.

10. Jack Kornfield, *A Path With Heart: A Guide Through the Perils and Promises of Spiritual Life* (New York: Bantam Books, 1993), p. 164.

11. Claire Myers Owens, in Charles T. Tart, *Transpersonal Psychologies: Perspectives on the Mind From Seven Great Spiritual Traditions* (San Francisco: HarperSanFrancisco, 1992), p. 156.

12. Ibid, p. 168.

Chapter 9: *Mindfulness*

Epigraph 1: Charles Tart, *Living the Mindful Life: A Handbook for Living in the Present Moment* (Boston: Shambhala Publications, Inc., 1994), p. 41.

Epigraph 2: Keen, *Life*, p. 135–137.

1. Alan Watts, *Talking Zen* (New York: Weatherhill Inc., 1994, p. 45.

2. Thich Nhat Hanh, *Living Buddha, Living Christ* (New York: Riverhead Books, 1995), p. 116–17.

3. Stephen Levine, *A Gradual Awakening* (New York: Anchor Books, 1979), p. 29.

Chapter 10: *Stations of the Cross*

Epigraph 1: Thomas à Kempis, *The Imitation of Christ* (London: Penguin Books, 1952), p. 86.

Epigraph 2: Matthew Fox, *The Coming of the Cosmic Christ* (San Francisco: HarperSanFranciso, 1988), p. 139.

1. Anthony de Mello, *The Heart of the Enlightened* (New York: Image Books, 1991), p. 184.

2. Anthony de Mello, *One Minute Nonsense* (Chicago: Loyola University Press, 1992), p. 5.

3. de Mello, *Heart*, p. 186.

4. Ibid, p. 40.

5. Ibid, p. 41.

6. Anthony de Mello, *Nonsense*, p. 48.

7. Anthony de Mello, *Heart*, p. 161.

8. Brunton, *Ego*, p. 47.

9. Thomas Merton, *New Seeds* of Contemplation (New York: New Directions Books, 1972), 218–19.

10. de Mello, *Heart*, p. 190.

11. Ibid, p. 19.

12. Ibid, p.165.

13. Watts, *Talking Zen*, p. 137.

14. Quoted in Stephen Mitchell, ed., *The Enlightened Mind* (New York: HarperCollins Publishers, 1991), p. 34.

15. de Mello, *Heart*, p. 99.

Chapter 11: *Loving-Kindness*

Epigraph 1: I Corinthians 13:1

Epigraph 2: Armstrong, *History*, p. 279.

Chapter 12: *Facing Death*

Epigraph 1: Rinpoche, *Tibetan Book*, p. 8.

Epigraph 2: Philip Kapleau, *The Wheel of Life and Death: A Practical and Spiritual Guide* (New York: Anchor Books, 1989), p.59.

1. Larry Dossey quoted in Ted Braude, "The Reach of the Mind: An Interview With Larry Dossey," *Pathways: A Journal of Psychological and Spiritual Transformation*, Vol. 4, No. 3, p. 6.

2. Ibid, p. 6.

3. Bruce Langford, "A Eulogy," *Pathways: A Journal of Psychological and Spiritual Transformation,* Vol. 2, No. 3, April, 1993, p. 8.

4. Matthew 10:28

5. Quoted in Philip Kapleau, *The Wheel of Life and Death: A Practical Spiritual Guide* (New York: Anchor Books, 1989), p. 61

Chapter 13: *In Remembrance*

Epigraph 1: Romans 8:38–39.

Epigraph 2: Chuang Tzu, *The Complete Works of Chuang Tzu,* trans. Burton Watson (New York: Columbia University Press, 1968), p.47.

Chapter 14: *Resurrection*

Epigraph 1: I Corinthians 13:12.

Epigraph 2: *A Course in Miracles: Manual for Teachers* (Tiburon, California: Foundation for Inner Peace, 1985), p. 65.

1. J. Krishnamurti, *The Awakening of Intelligence* (San Francisco: HarperCollins Publishers, 1973), p. 195.

2. Becker, *Denial,* p. 26.

Chapter 15: *Forgiveness*

Epigraph 1: Tillich, *Being,* pp. 7–8.

Epigraph 2: *A Course in Miracles: Text,* p. 329.

Chapter 16: *A Gift of Faith*

Epigraph 1: Luke 6:32–36.

Epigraph 2: Thomas Merton, *The New Man* (New York: Farrar Straus Giroux, 1961), p. 190.

Chapter 17: *Mystical Wisdom*

Epigraph 1: William Kingsland, *The Gnosis or Ancient Wisdom in the Christian Scriptures* (London: George Allen & Unwin Ltd., 1937), pp. 47–48.

Epigraph 2: Alan Watts, *Behold the Spirit* (New York: Vintage Books, 1971), p. 55.

1. Genesis 15:2–6.

2. Their names are Abram and Sarai before the birth of Isaac. Then God changes their names to Abraham and Sarah—to symbolize spiritual transformation.

3. *Meister Eckhart.* Franz Pfeiffer, ed., 1857, translated by C. de B. Evans (London, John M. Watkins, third impression 1956), p.3.

4. Matthew Fox, *Breakthrough: Meister Eckhart's Creation Spirituality in New Translation* (New York: Image Books, 1980), p. 322.

5. Hanh, *Living Buddha,* p. 40

6. When Nicodemus, a member of the Jewish religious establishment, came to Christ by night to question him about spiritual matters, Jesus said to him, "Truly, truly, I say to you, unless one is born again, he cannot see the kingdom of God" (John 3:3, NASB)

Nicodemus interpreted this quite literally and asked Christ how it was possible that someone could return to their mother's womb and be born again. This same crude literalism characterizes the modern Christian conception of spiritual rebirth (which is greatly influenced by the Renaissance's inflation and near-deification of reason or discursive intellect and the Reformation's emphasis on literalism and doctrinal purity.

The intellectual acceptance of a body of doctrine and the cheerful allegiance to a system of moral precepts may well be a necessary prerequisite to the Christian life, just as physical birth is a *necessary* prerequisite for later spiritual development. These activities can surely help to reduce our fears and calm our minds so we can begin the process of inner exploration. But they are not *sufficient* conditions of our spiritual transformation. As Jesus told Nicodemus, "Truly, truly, I say to you, unless one is born of water *and* the Spirit, he cannot enter into the kingdom of God" (John 3:5, NASB). (See also John 1:13, I Peter 1:3, 23, I John 4:7, 5:1–4.)

What does it mean to be "born of the Spirit?" Again, scriptural literalists have variously interpreted this to mean that we must walk down a church aisle and "accept Jesus," or we must "speak in tongues," or be "baptized in the Spirit," or perform some other visible and concrete behavior that will give testimony to our new birth. None of these events is anything more than an initial step on the journey.

The Apostle Paul, perhaps the greatest single interpreter of the Gospel of Jesus Christ, wrote: *Be transformed by the renewing of your mind,* that you may prove what the will of God is, that which is good and acceptable and perfect" (Romans 12:2, NASB). Elsewhere he wrote, "*Let this mind be in you* which was also in Christ Jesus" (Philippians 2:5 KJVV). (See also I Corinthians 2:16.) This "second birth" or transformation of mind is a much deeper and more gradual process than our current teachings concerning salvation would imply. It is essentially identical to what is called "enlightenment" in Eastern religious traditions. It is true salvation.

7. Fox, *Breakthrough*, p. 329.

8. Philippians 2:5.

9. Philip Kapleau, *Zen: Merging of East and West* (New York: Anchor Books, 1989), p. 41.

10. Genesis 16:1–2.

11. Brunton, *Ego*, p. 100, p. 90.

12. Watts, *Happiness*, p. xix.

13. Genesis 16:7–10.

14. Romans 8:28.

15. Brendan Doyle, *Meditations with Julian of Norwich* (Santa Fe, New Mexico: Bear & Co., 1983), p. 39.

Afterword

1. Merton, *New Seeds*, p. 159.

ABOUT THE AUTHOR

Richard G. Young, Ph.D. is a licensed psychotherapist who has been in private practice for the past eighteen years. He currently serves as Clinical Director of Pathways Counseling Center in Riverside, California, a multi-disciplinary psychotherapy group specializing in counseling from an integrative and spiritual perspective. His therapeutic specialties include individual, marital, and family counseling, transpersonal psychotherapy, and the integration of psychology and spirituality.

Dr. Young is also Director of the Center for Contemplative Christianity in Riverside, California. This ecumenical organization is dedicated to rediscovering the meditative and mystical tradition within the Christian faith by entering into authentic and mutually respectful dialogue with other religious traditions. Members and students of the Center attempt to explore the deeper aspects of their own spiritual lives through intensive study and regular meditation practice. Dr. Young also serves as Publisher of the Center's bi-monthly magazine.

Dr. Young spent thirteen years at California Baptist College, where he served as Associate Professor and Head of the Psychology Department and Director of Counseling. He is currently Adjunct Professor of Psychology at United States International University in San Diego, where he teaches in the doctoral program. He writes and lectures widely on transpersonal psychology and various aspects of the spiritual journey. He also leads *Vipassana* or insight meditation retreats in various parts of the country each year. He lives in Riverside with his wife, Nancy, and their two sons, Chad and Adam.

Information from the Author

More information is available from the author on the ideas brought forth in *Paths of a Prodigal*. You may subscribe to the bi-monthly magazine written by Richard Young and several other indentured servants entitled, *Pathways: A Magazine of Psychological and Spiritual Transformation*. This magazine is an ecumenical experiment in love and faith that attempts to serve and encourage those who are on the path of deeper spiritual understanding.

If you are interested in subscribing to *Pathways* and receiving regular information about Dr. Young's insight meditation retreats, seminars, and other programs, the yearly subscription price (six issues) is only $21.95.

Also available from Dr. Young is an audio tape entitled, *Stages of the Mystical Journey*, for $8.95 and a two-tape set entitled, *Four Guided Meditations*. These meditations are based on those found in *Paths of a Prodigal* and are read by Richard Young and Bruce Langford. They sell for only $15.95.

Indicate what you would like to order and mail a check or money order in the proper amount to:

Pathways Publications and Seminars
P.O. Box 2330, Riverside, California 92516